TEACHING

the

VIRTUES

NOTE FROM THE PUBLISHER

Everything starts with a book, according to a saying in publishing.
I don't know about *everything*, but books shape intellectual and cultural milieus. Books built American conservatism, for example.

That is why the Russell Kirk Center is excited to announce Mecosta House, a new publishing imprint. Mecosta House is dedicated to promulgating the legacy of Russell Kirk, and the tradition he articulated from his beloved Piety Hill in his ancestral village of Mecosta, from which we take our name.

Our mission is rooted in reverence for the Permanent Things—those timeless principles and moral norms that uphold the family, religion, private property, schools, and the social bonds and associations that, as Edmund Burke wrote, hold us together in a partnership between the living, the dead, and those yet to be born.

At Mecosta House, we hope to foster a community of readers and thinkers dedicated to exploring the wisdom of our predecessors while forging a new conservative humanism. Our catalog will include explorations of Burkean conservative thought, moral imagination, historical consciousness, political prudence, community, human anthropology, literature, humane economics, education, and liberty under law—all in light of the Permanent Things. We aim to give each new generation access to the beliefs, practices, and institutions that are the foundation of America's constitutional achievement in ordered liberty.

We are proud to present David Hein's engaging *Teaching the Virtues* as our first book. In the future, we will publish new editions of classic works by Russell Kirk, a series or two, some fiction, essay collections, and new works in the old tradition.

Welcome home to Mecosta House!

Jeffrey O. Nelson, PhD
Publisher

Praise for *Teaching the Virtues*

"Impressively well read in ethics, theology, history, and educational theory, Professor Hein is uniquely equipped to write this very important book, which needs to be read by anyone interested in teaching the virtues in secondary schools."
—The Reverend Dr. D. Stuart Dunnan,
    headmaster of Saint James School (Maryland)

"*Teaching the Virtues* is a gateway. Enter it for useful and hopeful thoughts about teaching, learning, and life."
—Richard Brookhiser, author of *George Washington on Leadership*

"Historically informed, immensely practical, and morally compelling, this book is a tonic for an age that regards the old virtues with contempt."
—Joseph Loconte, C. S. Lewis Scholar for
    Public Life at Grove City College

"This primer on teaching virtue will serve teachers and nonteachers interested in living well and helping others to live well."
—Mark Tooley, president of the
    Institute on Religion and Democracy

"Anyone who has pondered such questions as 'How should I live my life?' will be grateful to David Hein for this scintillating and accessible trip through the garden of practical wisdom."
—Roger Kimball, editor of the *New Criterion*

"What a joy and privilege it is to read and reflect on this eloquent and timely new book! Hein is a scholarly historian, biographer, cultural commentator, and teacher extraordinaire."
—The Very Reverend William Noble McKeachie,
    dean emeritus of the Diocese of South Carolina

"This elegantly constructed primer on teaching virtues is a *must read* for all parents of school-age children."
—C. Russell Fletcher III, chairman emeritus
    of the George C. Marshall Foundation

"In an age of moral vacuity and anomie, *Teaching the Virtues* is a timely, edifying, and inspiring book."
　—George H. Nash, historian, senior fellow at the
　　Russell Kirk Center for Cultural Renewal

"Elegantly written with clarity and a reluctant (because humble) authority, this beautiful little book offers the distilled wisdom of decades in the classroom, broad reading, and deep reflection. It begins a conversation among educators regarding the ethical character on which true learning depends."
　—Ryan R. Holston, Jonathan Myrick Daniels '61 Chair for
　　Academic Excellence at the Virginia Military Institute

"Dr. Hein's book provides much matter for thought, and subsequent action, for educators and parents to intentionally transfer a culture of virtue to the young."
　—Alvaro de Vicente, headmaster of
　　The Heights School for Boys, Potomac, Maryland

"By introducing the reader to the 'permanent things,' Hein illustrates the importance of teaching the enduring truths found in arts and letters in order to form students virtuously."
　—Lee Trepanier, dean of the D'Amour College of
　　Liberal Arts and Sciences at Assumption University

"In an age of moral discord and cultural transition, this brief, discerning, and supremely engaging work will appeal to all who have sought to comprehend their standing in the moral universe and to communicate that quest and understanding to others."
　—Philip Terzian, author of *Architects of Power:
　　Roosevelt, Eisenhower, and the American Century*

"David Hein's little book is a treasure. It is a brilliant exposition of educational philosophy and an argument about how, in the classroom, teaching writing can cultivate virtue—and how good writing can itself be an exercise in virtue."
　—Vigen Guroian, author of *Tending the Heart of Virtue*

TEACHING

the

VIRTUES

DAVID HEIN

MECOSTA
HOUSE

Mecosta, Michigan

ISBN 979-8-9926395-9-9

LCCN on file with the Library of Congress

Published in the United States by
Mecosta House
The imprint of the Russell Kirk Center for Cultural Renewal
Mecosta, Michigan

The Russell Kirk Center for Cultural Renewal aims to recover, conserve, and enliven those enduring norms and principles that Russell Kirk (1918–1994) called the Permanent Things.

Manufactured in the United States of America

Cover design by Δlek

Cover photo courtesy of Saint James School (Hagerstown, Maryland) and Kim Dudash

To our students

CONTENTS

FOREWORD

_____   _____

by Roberta L. Bayer

On a recent visit to a historic boarding school in western Maryland, I happened to notice a young man emerging from his residence with his guitar. Sitting down in a tranquil spot to practice, he offered a perfect picture of quiet concentration. He was absorbed in an occupation that was both beautiful and attentive. Another day, I saw a student sitting cross-legged on the floor outside my faculty office. He was patiently reading, engrossed in a book. I remember these scenes because they are so rare these days, even though the virtues of attention, self-discipline, and piety are the means to happiness.

This book, *Teaching the Virtues*, will inspire teachers in Christian schools. It is about creating an educational culture in which students learn such habits as attention in study, courage in the face of challenges, and graciousness in winning and losing. Its thesis is that young people learn virtue by *becoming*

persons of good character. Character is the outcome of education of the mind and habituation of the will. This is not a radical idea; it is an old idea, true to human nature.

In 1776, John Adams wrote, "All sober inquirers after truth,
ancient and modern, pagan and Christian, have declared that
the happiness of man, as well as his dignity, consists in virtue." He believed that the fate of the American experiment in
republican government would depend on this knowledge: happiness, political freedom, and the exercise of virtue are insepa-
rable. Laws should inspire citizens to the dignity of freemen,
to good humor and sociability, to good manners and morals.
To encourage public and private virtue within the citizenry,
Adams commended both sumptuary laws, which restrict lux-
uries and extravagance, and liberal education for youth.

In an era in which influential men and women say that individuals have the right to define their own ethics and identities,
Adams's observations may be perplexing, even objectionable.
How can it be that the moral habits of citizens are necessary to
political liberty? Are not individual rights enough?

David Hein answers no, and he does so by arguing for the
importance of uniting virtue with education. Writing an essay
requires moral virtue, so instructors should teach students this
fact. Plagiarism is harmful to another person, for it is an act of
theft and deception. These and other examples of how to teach
virtue are persuasively set before the reader.

An education should form both character and mind, and
instill good judgment in the young before they are faced with
morally complex situations. It should also introduce young
people to the "permanent things," in T. S. Eliot's phrase: permanent truths, found not only in math and science but also in
morals and metaphysics. It should teach the theological virtues, the cardinal virtues, and such good traits as kindness,

generosity, humility, gratitude, piety, loyalty, and integrity. Professor Hein's book tells us why.

The ordinary person may presume that whatever he or she thinks is right and leave it at that. But in their hearts, most people know, for all the lip service they give to the nostrums of the age, that this belief is not true. Almost all students recognize when they are treated unkindly or unjustly by others. Their experience should prompt a new thought: what is it to behave well? To this question an answer should be given. Abstract moral theories are fine for the academically inclined, but high school students require practical instruction.

The purpose of education is indicated by the Latin word *educere*, to lead out. An educator leads a student out of ignorance into truth. Plato, the ancient Greek philosopher who lived four centuries before Christ, famously offered the following allegory to explain the nature of education.

Lack of learning is like sitting in darkness at the bottom of a cave. Education is the experience of being led out of that cave, moving from darkness to light, in the course of which, when turning from the shadows to the light of day, a person comes to see that what was formerly believed to be true is in fact false—and with this knowledge of reality and truth comes happiness. Virtue and knowledge and freedom from ignorance bring well-being, or *eudaimonia*, the Greek word for happiness, which means good character, human excellence and flourishing, a well-ordered soul.

As Plato's Allegory of the Cave suggests, this goal is not attained without a teacher, someone to guide the student out of the cave and into the light. This fact is why schools are communities of learning. For it is not only through an excellent curriculum but also through the practice of excellence that the best schools foster an environment of virtue.

This unusual little book will not make anyone more virtuous. But this primer—written with conviction, in strong and clear prose—will help instructors, coaches, and school leaders to think about and teach the ancient virtues much more knowledgeably and effectively. Our culture urgently needs everything that this distinctive work represents.

Roberta L. Bayer
Patrick Henry College
Purcellville, Virginia

TEACHING
THE VIRTUES

This short book requires little by way of an introduction, let alone a summary of its contents. But the reader might benefit from a word or two of orientation. Unlike most authors, I urge you not only to agree or disagree with what I say in these pages but also to rewrite this book as you go along. Especially when I discuss teaching the virtues, I am well aware that you know far more about your students, your schools, and your subjects than I do.

My examples—in Parts 1 and 2—are inferior to what you can come up with. Far from being offended if you rewrite my paragraphs, I would be disappointed if you did not repeatedly do so. I would find it most gratifying if you entered into the spirit of this enterprise by producing another book, a unique text parallel to but better than this one: a book more appropriate to your classroom and your experience.

The other clue to what I have in mind is that both halves of this book deal with teaching the virtues. Both offer various examples. But the first half is weighted toward discussion of schools, and the second half toward discussion of the virtues. The purpose of the second half is to give teachers more material to consider and possibly to teach regarding the virtues. But the first half also incorporates discussion of the virtues, and the second half also talks about teaching and schools.

Part 2 expands the discussion of the virtues first by presenting ways to complicate these traits of good character, making your discussion of them more challenging and therefore more interesting for your pupils. It also expands on what is offered in Part 1 by adding to the beginning list of seven virtues and by discussing illustrations from history, literature, and film. Just as the second half adds some virtues—such as gratitude, stability, patience, a sense of duty, integrity, loyalty, and piety—so should you feel free to add and explore your own choices.

This is not a book about the virtues. Nor is it a book about teaching. Excellent texts on each of these subjects are easy to find. This book is a primer on teaching the virtues.

Who, then, is the reader for this book? First, I have in mind teachers at traditional church schools, in classical Christian schools, and in homeschooling settings. Teachers I address directly in this book. Second, I hope that these chapters will be of interest to school leaders, parents, and perhaps even a few students.

Can Virtue Be Taught?

As a primer on teaching the virtues, this book raises the question of whether the virtues can be taught. You might ask your students—like many thinkers before them—to consider this problem. Or, even better, ask this larger question: How can a person become virtuous? By being informed of what the virtues are, including definitions and examples? By studying good role models? By absorbing stories about fine people? By lending a hand in a service project? By attending church regularly? By reading the Bible? By grace alone?

To the question *Can virtue be taught?* my response is not a simple yes. I think instead of a circle or ring with three equidistant faculties positioned around the circumference: Cognition (at 0°, if you like), Volition (120°), and Action (240°). Emotion I imagine always buzzing in the background. My unscientific theory is that becoming virtuous involves all three functions: learning and thinking, willing, and acting. A kind of hermeneutical circle, it can be entered at any point, and what you gain from one faculty should reinforce the next capacity, all conducing to the establishment of a good habit.

As the Christian educator Hannah More observed, the acquisition of a virtue typically requires the eradication of a vice. A cigarette smoker in my late teens and early twenties, I knew (at some level) that I wanted to do right by myself (justice), I sought self-control (temperance), I desired a long and healthy life (hope), I didn't want to keep being foolish (prudence), I wished to be strong and not weak (fortitude), and so forth. Most of all, I wanted to be free and no longer the slave of my addiction.

Of course, my will was conflicted (I also wanted to smoke), my mind was torn (it said I would quit soon; this was my last pack; I'll stop after I get through this big paper or final exam; what harm would one more do me?), and my actions reflected ambivalence (purchasing supposedly less-harmful smokes and fewer of them; substituting begging for buying; etc.). As a

backdrop to this dilemma, emotions were unhelpfully com-
municating both satisfaction (my pleasure) and shame (my
weakness).

As More counseled, first I needed to eradicate the vice.
The goal in view was to end the addiction and to recover wind
and lung tissue. Therefore the action sought was quitting and
staying quit. My sense is that both cognition and volition were
crucial in the process of quitting. Once, when I had a bad case
of bronchitis and went to Student Health, the medical resident
asked me whether I smoked. I answered yes but that I was trying to quit.

Quietly and calmly, the young physician supported my
effort by telling me that he'd just been attending patients in
the University Hospital and one of them was dying of COPD:
chronic obstructive pulmonary disease. He said emphysema
was a bad way to go. As you can see, I've never forgotten his
simple, straightforward statement. It unquestionably strength-
ened my determination to break the habit. But knowledge by
itself was not enough. It took me another three years following
that appointment to take decisive action.

In other words, I am for throwing everything—not just
teaching or preaching—at this problem of realizing one's best
self. As Chapter 1 will (I hope) make clear, I think it's a big
mistake either to avoid clear and explicit discussion of the traditional virtues or to confine mention of them to one place and
time. I introduce a metaphor that recommends engaging the
virtues all around the circle of students' activities.

Even then, everything will depend on the motivation and
effort of the individual student. Ultimately, formation is his
or her responsibility. No one can become a man or a woman
for someone else. Although friends and family members were
supportive, no one could quit smoking for me.

Is anyone wholly virtuous for even one day? Few individuals are consistently patient, generous, or loving. As we shall find in Chapter 5, the theologian H. Richard Niebuhr points out that Christians' faith—that is, the faith of actual, not theoretical or ideal, Christians—more closely resembles henotheism than monotheism: in the course of a week, we blithely bow down before many gods. We fail and fall short again and again. Which is where the last chapter, on the virtue of piety, comes in.

Part 1

SCHOOLS

1

POLITICS AND
BALL BEARINGS

The difference between being educated and being schooled is the difference between being equipped to ride a horse across open country and being led on horseback around a ring.

Merely being schooled can take place in any academic institution. The core problem of this limited—and limiting—experience is its failure fully to engage heart and mind. The reason for this deficiency is schooling's muddled mission, coupled with self-deception: its practitioners' conviction that they know what they're doing, and that what they're doing constitutes "best practices."

Both school leaders and their constituents need to step back from strategic plans, assessment devices, external reviews, competitive rankings, diversity definitions, and formulaic mission statements for the sake of posing straightforward questions about vision and effectiveness.

Imagine that a mother and a father, looking out for the best interests of their son or daughter, are attracted by a church-affiliated school. Appreciating this school's commitment to nurturing each child's whole self, these parents seek answers to the following questions:

Given that this institution's raison d'être is the development of each student's body, soul, and intellect, are this school's promises being realized? Do its programs, including required chapel services and classes in religious education, not only meet high standards but also enable all students to reach their full potential? Are young scholars sparked by what's on offer, finding their way in widening fields of knowledge and endeavor, or are they simply going through the motions, performing acceptably or even admirably, as they are led around the academic ring? Is sound moral and spiritual formation likely to occur? In brief, are intentions and processes in sync?

Most honest observers of schools, both secular and religious, would acknowledge a gap between what's sought and what's regularly accomplished. It's a fault that cannot be put down solely to adolescents' invariably incomplete, distracted natures or to teachers' inevitable failure to reach all their pupils all the time. No one is demanding academic utopia, but even very good schools can do better.

Which is where those of us who care about raising up young people as beneficiaries and trustees of the treasures of Western civilization might proffer a notion: In thinking about these little educational platoons, consider invoking some concepts from the world of political theory. Which balance of individual, community, and nation is best for the commonweal? Which arrangement of order, justice, and liberty is most propitious both for the good of each citizen and for the general welfare?

Conservative Liberalism

Conservative liberalism is a phrase that connotes both a realistic appraisal of human nature and a hopeful approach to human possibility. At its center, this political outlook incorporates a liberal understanding of fundamental human rights, including freedom of speech, freedom of association, and freedom of religion. It stands for equality before the law and equality before our Creator. It embraces equal opportunity and basic fairness. It acknowledges—indeed it celebrates—the right of all citizens to rise and to make something of themselves.

Conservatives grasp the truth that liberal values and policies, expressing individual liberty, are best understood not as abstractions derived from a theoretical social contract but as commitments and practices rooted in the rich cultural soil of Athens and Rome, of Jerusalem and London. Moreover, in the United States, we can see how—to cite two significant cases—freedom's distinctive character has been forged not only by the realistic hopes of eighteenth-century Philadelphia, Pennsylvania, but also by the annealing tragedies of twentieth-century Philadelphia, Mississippi.

If the latter Philadelphia, a town of seven thousand residents, is not as well known today as the northern City of Brotherly Love, then this fact can remind us to comprehend liberalism—both its historical origins and its contemporary existence—in relation not only to famous cities of the Western world but also to the tens of thousands of more modest communities spread across this land. In conurbations and towns and hamlets, as well as in families, schools, and civic enterprises, our experiences teach us that liberty flourishes when joined with forbearance.

Habits of moral excellence are necessary if a free republic

is to prosper. As Benjamin Franklin averred, "Only a virtuous people are capable of freedom." Freedom succeeds when influenced by habits of the heart that incline citizens toward temperance and patience, toward justice and mutual respect, rather than toward selfish opportunism, willful violence, or the divisive ideologies of race or class. Conservative liberalism is bounded and informed by tradition, which comprises the accretions of practical wisdom and worthwhile experience over time. And prescription—long-established, authoritative custom—is ever open to prudent reform.

The imagination of the conservative liberal, therefore, is enlivened by virtue, not deadened by vice. This moral imagination is nurtured by the best that has been thought and written in ethics, literature, and theology. It is a historical imagination, tethered to reality, to lived experience in community, rather than a fancy that drifts off in clouds of wishful thinking or heedless egocentrism. Notwithstanding manifest differences between them, the following thinkers may be taken as representative of this political outlook: Edmund Burke, Alexis de Tocqueville, Michael Oakeshott, Raymond Aron, Russell Kirk, and Roger Scruton.

The most salubrious option for the polity at large, conservative liberalism is also the most fitting and helpful, the most workable and inspiring, stance for schools today. Developmentally, boys and girls are still molten creatures, their judgment unsteady and their opinions unsettled. Within the limits of civility, students must be free to raise questions and to voice doubts. As Professor Caroline Breashears asserts in *Law & Liberty*, "It is essential to allow challenges to the truth so that it can be supported rationally." Pupils should enjoy freedom of expression, necessary for academic inquiry and for forming reasoned positions.

Not only state schools but also traditional church foundations omit religious litmus tests in admissions; they believe in freedom of religious belief. Neither at my alma mater, St. Paul's School in Brooklandville, Maryland, nor at the school I am honored to serve as a trustee, Saint James School near Hagerstown, Maryland, are students required to be Anglicans. Muslims, Jews, Hindus, Buddhists, and even Baptists have happily attended both institutions. In no school is militant woke fundamentalism or militant Christian fundamentalism desirable as either policy or practice.

In a church school, if a student wishes to raise questions about the role of a loving God in the face of a devastating natural disaster such as an earthquake, then good for her. If a student feels compelled to confess that, following the death of his little sister to bone cancer, he is having trouble believing in an active, benevolent Creator, then he should be supported in admitting this fact. If a student has questions about the Trinity—about how God can be three Persons (*hypostases*) in one divine essence (*ousia*)—then, unabashedly, she should ask them. If her senior-year colleague wants to know how in Jesus Christ, the incarnate Word, one Person can exist in two natures, human and divine, without either confusion or separation, then he should calmly put his question and not be made to feel an outcast. These students' teachers might assure their charges that learned theologians have been pondering these mysteries as well, and for quite some time. As Professor Breashears observes, "If we never discuss a doctrine, we lose its meaning."

By the same token, if a student feels led to question the ethics or theology surrounding gay marriage, then she should be allowed to speak up, without facing accusations of "hate." If another student desires to challenge the wisdom of prescribing puberty blockers for children, he should not be scorned. If his classmate wishes to dispute the moral and historical reasoning behind demands for "reparations," she should not be ostracized. If her conscientious peer feels compelled to express skepticism in response to claims of "systemic racism," he should not be branded a racist for voicing his doubts.

Within the shared setting of intellectual inquiry, the atmosphere should be conducive, as Oakeshott says, to conversation, which needs to be respectful, charitable, patient, nonviolent, noncoercive—and free. Hence each school—like the best colleges—must have a liberal grounding.

At the same time, each school should make it clear what it holds to be true belief and right conduct. Church schools—such as Saint James—strike me as the freest of all. Within their walls, students and teachers may openly affirm both Darwin's theory of evolution by natural selection and the writings of C. S. Lewis. At the best schools, no ideology is imposed, no rigid conformity enforced.

The problem that arises, however, is the poor fit—sometimes appearing as friction, sometimes as disconnect—between inner freedom and outer structure, between individual liberty and institutional tradition. Church schools have much to offer, but they have trouble meshing church and school. How can an academic community integrate the two? Required chapel segregates Christianity in one time and space. A theology or church history course can be valuable, but it is only one class—and typically not viewed as the most important one—in a rich schedule comprising academics, athletics, and the arts.

Courses in world religions are informative, also, but they can imply a relativistic attitude toward all faiths, according to which nonjudgmental pluralism (testified to by the COEXIST bumper sticker) is viewed not as a problem but as the ideal. The opposite position, dogmatic religious exclusivism, would strike most teenaged students as epistemologically impossible and downright unfriendly.

Ball Bearings

The political analogy of conservative liberalism is useful, but it takes us only so far in our thinking toward the best scholastic constitution within a highly competitive and pluriform educational environment. Therefore we might weigh the merits of another intervention: a complementary analogy borrowed from the world not of political theory but of mechanical efficiency. Such metaphors are common. The post–World War II European Recovery Program—the Marshall Plan—was conceptually hard to grasp. For many ordinary citizens, the images of pump primer and industrial lubricant made this program's economic purpose and function more intelligible.

Keeping in mind the sticking points mentioned above, imagine a traditional church school. Now picture ball bearings. This sort of rolling-element bearing uses metal balls to separate two concentric rings. Each ring contains a groove in which the balls rest. The result is a mechanism that reduces friction across moving planes. By limiting surface contact, the bearing rings ease motion. Otherwise, too much rubbing against moving parts would impede the device's action.

In a church school, the axle around which everything rolls is the students, always at the center.

The inner ring is the whole panoply of classes and chapel, games and the arts, extracurriculars and outings, rules and punishments, papers and labs and exams, together with

Ball bearings, assembled (above) and disassembled (below)

correction and encouragement. All enhance learning within an environment conducive to ordered freedom and thus to moral, intellectual, artistic, athletic, and personal development.

The outer ring should be the school's most profound commitments and character—its ethos as an orthodox Christian institution, its participation in the sacraments, its trust in and loyalty to Christ, not idols. This outer, conservative ring is a safeguard against faddism. While contributing to the institution's forward movement, it steadies the school, keeping it true to its heritage and to its essential nature.

Without the balls separating the tool rings, the outer ring would bear down too hard on the inner ring and the axle, imperiling free movement. The balls prevent this breakdown from happening. At the same time, they maintain good contact all around the inner ring. What are the metal balls in a church school? Where may be found the necessary parts that the conservative-liberal analogy leaves out? Discovering answers to these questions requires exploration by way of curiosity, humility, and affinity: a course of thought and action that goes beyond participating in workshops on "best practices."

Scholastic Ecumenism

Within our highly variegated culture, traditional schools must negotiate the inclines, dips, and curves of multilane academic highways. Families have numerous options to choose from: public charter schools, progressive schools, specialized schools in the arts or in science and technology, classical academies, traditional boarding schools, historic day schools, evangelical Christian schools, homeschooling, Roman Catholic schools, Quaker schools, and others. On behalf of their children (a school's clients), parents (a school's customers) avidly seek the largest return on their investment.

The choices are many and various, and all schools want to flourish. In this milieu, how can a tradition-oriented school discover its crucial interactive components and its path to prosperity? The answer lies along a route marked by those who have thought about the aims and approaches of ecumenism.

The species of ecumenism that most of us are familiar with strives toward agreements between theologically aligned communions on such matters as baptism, justification, the Lord's Supper, and the historic episcopate. This approach typically has as its ultimate aim settling differences of faith and polity to achieve full communion.

In an article in *First Things*, Cardinal Avery Dulles discusses an appealing alternative—or complement—to this convergence model: receptive ecumenism, which does not seek full communion or even agreement. Rather, its aim is reform within: listening to and learning from another ecclesial body so that positive change—spiritual renewal—can occur within one's church.

Leaders of traditional church schools might benefit from being receptive to developments beyond their home institutions, particularly where meaningful affinities exist.

Many schools represent their understanding of mission through the head's public statements and letters to the community from leading administrators. But what is usually missing is the involvement of *all* the faculty in interpreting their school's ethos. For example, an upper-school Classics instructor might reflect on how his teaching of *Plutarch's Lives* offers a compelling story- and character-driven way to study history.

That's just what you'll find at The Heights, a Roman Catholic boys' school in Potomac, Maryland, near the nation's capital. In a podcast interview for his school's online *Heights Forum*, veteran humanities teacher Tom Cox enthusiastically discloses how "boys come alive" when they confront the difficulties faced by great leaders, such as Cicero, and discern the influence these figures had on our country's founders. Through these examples, students learn about flawed but still inspiring human beings who displayed virtue amid their struggles.

By means of this teacher's thoughtful take on his work—his elucidation of "why and how we teach Plutarch"—listeners augment their understanding of The Heights, its goals and methods. Experiencing a purposeful academic enterprise, they recognize what this school is attempting to achieve in the education of "young men fully alive in the liberal-arts tradition."

Classical Christian schools (CCSs) offer much that the rest of us should assess with an eye to reforming our enterprises. In the spirit of receptive ecumenism, those of us associated with much older schools should be open to learning from those whose institutional practices dovetail with our convictions but flesh out our principles in ways we might have overlooked. Certainly, CCSs have borrowed from traditional educators: they love the works of Dorothy L. Sayers (paying close attention to *The Lost Tools of Learning*) and C. S. Lewis (especially *The Abolition of Man*).

Two features of the CCS program are particularly relevant to our concerns in this chapter: *integration* and *virtues*. The CCS literature notes that academic subjects are too separated in most schools, both public and independent. Each discipline is a smokestack by itself. If there's a religion program, it tends to be represented almost exclusively in chapel or in one religious education course. Thus a gap exists between the regular academic subjects at most independent schools and any theological convictions the school has.

The other key element is that CCSs, with their classical and Christian commitments, emphasize the virtues, sharply distinguishing them from merely subjective values. They focus on the cardinal virtues of prudence, justice, courage, and temperance, and the theological virtues of faith, hope, and love. A leading text for CCS educators is *The Liberal Arts Tradition: A Philosophy of Christian Classical Education*, by Kevin Clark and Ravi Scott Jain. Its authors see the school as "a community of belief and practice that is striving toward virtue."

Truth, Goodness, and Persuasion

Traditional church schools have always stressed the will and the conscience, but they could be more thorough and focused in teaching about the virtues. The metal balls that enable the best interaction between institutional identity and diurnal activity are these habits of moral and spiritual excellence. They represent ways to bring transcendent norms into contact with teaching and coaching across each institution and in a manner that preserves freedom and propels personal growth. They are particularly appropriate for conservative-liberal schools, for, as a recent president of the Catholic University of America, John H. Garvey, points out, "The virtues are habits that channel our freedom in the direction we ought to go."

Schools must make a concerted effort to build and to maintain this mechanism, a rolling-element bearing with the ancient virtues mediating between students' freedom and the institution's faith. And schools must do so in the face of a popular culture in which such good habits as temperance, patience, humility, and gratitude are not the popular virtues. Instead, young people are bombarded with encouragements to salute creativity, individual expression, health and fitness, personal happiness, and some vague notions of social justice.

The rudiments of the traditional virtues should be apparent, however, to anyone who sets foot on the campus of a church school. Visitors to chapel will still hear these virtues preached. But outside of chapel, the curriculum often does not explicitly underscore and integrate the ancient virtues.

Church schools would benefit from being intentional and systematic in unpacking and analyzing the cardinal and the theological virtues, as well as such character traits as patience and humility, duty and gratitude. They should make it clear from the start and at regular intervals thereafter what "virtue" means. Otherwise their charges and most of their faculty will have no clear and consistent idea of what this word denotes: virtues are good habits conducing to good ends.

Through concrete examples, teachers and coaches can make the ancient virtues come alive. In his classic work *The Ethics of Rhetoric*, Richard M. Weaver limns exactly what this effort involves. In his opening chapter, he interprets Plato's dialogue *Phaedrus*. Weaver distinguishes the functions of dialectic and rhetoric. Dialectic is an inquiry that establishes the truth concerning some question. The good rhetorician is a lover of truth and therefore will offer no rhetoric without dialectic. But neither will the honest rhetorician persuade others to love what is true unless rhetoric completes dialectic. As Weaver observes, the result of dialectic on its own tends to be overly dry and abstract, too airy and disconnected from our ordinary lives. The rhetorician who depends solely on dialectic cannot incline his or her listeners toward a demonstrably true claim, such as the worth of justice.

Robert Penn Warren provides a memorable example of such a misfire in his novel *All the King's Men* (discussed at some length in Chapter 7). At the beginning of his career as a political stump speaker, the protagonist, Willie Stark, tries to convince his listeners by delivering addresses full of facts and figures and logic. Failing to connect with these local farmers and merchants, he cannot move them to support him and his cause, which is right and just. Eventually he does learn how to make this connection, rousing audiences with his dynamic speeches, and his political career is launched, even as his relationship to justice becomes more tenuous.

Although rhetoric incorporates dialectic, rhetoric must go beyond dialectic, for, as almost everyone realizes—and conservatives in particular have stressed—the complete person does not subsist in the land of theory alone but unites in his or her life thought, feeling, will, and action. Yes, the concept of justice is hard to grasp, but providing an audience with a practical illustration—"If someone owes you a debt, is it good for that person to pay you back?"—will provide a stepping stone to the larger truth. As Weaver points out, because rhetoric "has a passion for the actual," it can realize the ends of dialectic and, as it were, close the deal. That is why Plato often follows his conceptual analysis with a striking story.

Weaver observes that the human being "is a creature of passion and must live out that passion in the world." Surely, well-adjusted teenagers are eager to discover their passions and live them out in the world. Through sound rhetoric, their teachers can awaken their imaginations by helping them to picture this future, where virtues, which connect being and acting, do not detract from life's enjoyment but rather lie at the heart of a flourishing existence. Rhetoric may help a listener to look beyond a troubled present toward a brighter future—as Prime Minister Winston Churchill did during the darkest days of the Second World War. The reality was that Britons were struggling through, in Weaver's phrase, "a valley of humiliation." But Churchill addressed His Majesty's subjects and likened the future of Europe to "broad sunlit uplands," thus moving his countrymen's hearts and accomplishing through his rhetoric the most significant act of his premiership.

A little effort and imagination, responsibly deployed, can incite real commitment. Rhetoric grounds dialectic, relating it to the diurnal round. Teachers and coaches, therefore, should directly link the virtues to what students are doing and studying and thinking about, to their passions. Schools can do better than touching on these topics for some of their students some of the time. They should reach all their students nearly all the time. Then the substance of the virtues will become not bare and theoretical but instead truths to live by.

The Natural Necessity of Deep Roots

Is there anything arbitrary about choosing the traditional virtues to play the crucial interactive role between the interior (liberal) bearing ring and the outer (conservative) ring? Might metal balls of a different composition serve just as well? The answers to these questions are no and apparently not.

When I told one of my intelligent and well-educated neighbors that I was doing some work on the virtues, he characterized these traits as "lofty." Certainly the virtues have a transcendent dimension, but they are not ethereal. Essentially, they are quite down to earth, as the philosopher Philippa Foot establishes so well in her book *Natural Goodness*.

The virtues aim at realizing the good for each person. An oak tree has a good, which is survival and propagation. To achieve its purpose, the oak tree must have deep and sturdy roots. If it has the shallow root system of a creeping vine, then a strong wind will uproot it. The oak tree will perish, for it cannot bend like a reed. For human beings, the virtues are like the oak tree's deep, sturdy roots. They enable survival, propagation, and the realization of our distinctive ends.

Foot writes that men and women must be able to house, clothe, and feed themselves. They need to be able to form ties with family, friends, and neighbors. Within the larger society, they need laws. "And how," Foot asks, "could they have all these things without virtues such as loyalty, fairness, kindness, and in certain circumstances obedience?"

The virtues are what enable human beings to achieve their good ends: living in society, loving others, being reliable contributors. Within their own microcosms, students can infer the meaning and contribution of virtue from the fact that they can leave personal items like laptop computers lying around and no one will steal them. The more pervasive integrity is, the more both individuals and their companions can relax and flourish: freedom and forbearance growing together.

In *The Virtues*, the philosopher Peter Geach provides an arresting analogy: "Men need virtues as bees need stings." Both virtues in the lives of human beings and stingers in the lives of bees are natural and necessary. As Cicero says in *On the Laws*, "Virtue is nothing other than [nature] fully developed and taken all the way to its highest point."

Put that way, what student could resist the challenge? Who would want to turn down the adventure the virtues offer?

2

THE PRACTICAL
EDUCATION OF
THE YOUNG

Can virtue be taught?

Through the centuries, thinkers and teachers have proposed different answers to this fundamental question.

Some analysts of the problem suggest that the answer is no. Even the worthiest teachers and the finest texts cannot produce commitment in obstinate hearts, they maintain.

Others reject this view. In Plato's *Meno*, for example, Socrates says that virtue is a kind of knowledge and therefore can be taught.

Still others answer the question with a qualified yes. Virtue, they say, has more to do with the formation of good habits over time than with "knowledge" poured into the student. The conservative thinker Russell Kirk spoke for many when he asserted that virtue cannot be imparted directly, but outstanding literature can help shape persons into virtuous selves.

How a school and its leaders answer this question profoundly shapes the education the institution provides. Consider the Episcopal clergymen who led the preeminent church schools in the United States in the nineteenth century. The biography of the most important and influential of all these school leaders proves instructive. Henry Augustus Coit (1830–1895), the first rector (headmaster) of St. Paul's School, in Concord, New Hampshire, was a saintly figure who accomplished much good. But his deficiencies show us what to avoid in the practical education of the young.

In brief, his strengths lay in the conservative part of the rolling-element bearing, not in its liberal aspect. Which is not to say that he failed as an instructor, let alone as his school's longtime rector. No, he could be lucid and penetrating. But his methods were excessively austere and therefore incomplete.

The Education of Henry A. Coit

Born in Wilmington, Delaware, on January 20, 1830, young Henry, the second of nine children of an Episcopal rector, attended a remarkable academic institution: the prototype—short-lived but effective—of all the church boarding schools in America. The Flushing Institute opened in the spring of 1828 on Long Island, New York. The Reverend William Augustus Muhlenberg (1796–1877), a true religious entrepreneur, founded it as a successor to the Round Hill School. That family boarding school near Northampton, Massachusetts, had opened in 1823.

To the Round Hill model of a school that functioned as a close-knit community, in which teachers acted as surrogate parents and both worked and lived with students, Muhlenberg added a crucial element, a core identity: a consistent and rigorous Christian life. Pupils at the Flushing Institute attended chapel services twice daily. They participated in a spiritual program rooted in a specific Christian tradition, that of the Episcopal Church.

Financial difficulties forced the institute to close in 1846. But before Muhlenberg's experiment folded, it had given rise to successful progeny, starting with the College of St. James, near Hagerstown, Maryland, in 1842. This school's founding bishop, William Rollinson Whittingham, had tried to lure Muhlenberg to Maryland as his venture's first rector. Instead, in 1843, Muhlenberg sent his principal assistant, the Reverend John Barrett Kerfoot, who had been a student at the Flushing Institute.

Henry Coit went from the Flushing Institute to the University of Pennsylvania. Later he served as a tutor in the household of Stephen Elliott, Episcopal bishop of Georgia. In the early 1850s, Coit became an instructor of Greek and Latin at the College of St. James. Following ordination to the priesthood, he undertook missionary work in the diocese of Albany, New York, establishing several new congregations in Clinton County between 1854 and 1856.

Then his moment arrived: the Boston physician George Cheyne Shattuck Jr., a professor of clinical medicine at Harvard Medical School, had a summer estate at Millville, two miles west of Concord, New Hampshire. There he founded a boys' school, which began operating in April 1856 with three lads in residence. Two of them were Shattuck's sons.

Dr. Shattuck chose the twenty-six-year-old Coit to lead this fledgling enterprise. Coit would serve as rector until February 5, 1895, when, worn out from his labors, he died at the age of sixty-five. By the close of his life and career, St. Paul's

School enrolled 345 boys and employed thirty-six masters. The leading historian of American boarding schools, James McLachlan, has commented that at the time of Coit's death, "he was acclaimed as a major force in American education, a sort of American version of Arnold of Rugby."

Dr. Shattuck also helped to launch the Church of the Advent in Boston and Shattuck–St. Mary's School in Faribault, Minnesota. He supported the establishment in the United States of two Anglican religious orders: the Society of St. Margaret and the Society of St. John the Evangelist (the Cowley Fathers). As these initiatives suggest, Shattuck was a High Churchman, as were Henry Coit, William R. Whittingham, and John B. Kerfoot. (Muhlenberg was more ambiguous, styling himself an "evangelical catholic.") Indeed, their educational works expressed their High Church beliefs. Historians of St. Paul's write of the moderate High Church-manship that prevailed at the school during Coit's years.

Adherents to the doctrine of baptismal regeneration, High Churchmen sought to construct an environment in which the grace conferred at baptism would be realized in a character gradually transformed through participation in the services of the *Book of Common Prayer* and through the spiritual disciplines of the Episcopal Church. In an antebellum culture strongly influenced by Protestant evangelicalism, with its emphasis on emotional conversion ("born-again") experiences, Shattuck and Coit, like Whittingham and Kerfoot before them and other High Churchmen after them, developed a school with a decidedly different program. The chapel, whose rites were designed to be aesthetically appealing and spiritually affecting, was the center of school life. At St. Paul's, boys attended services daily, and many of the school's masters were men in training for the ministry.

The Reverend Dr. Henry Augustus Coit, first rector of St. Paul's School

Coit was dedicated, devout, even unworldly. With mixed success, he attempted to instill his preference for simplicity and self-sacrifice in the sons of the urban elite: Morgans, Mellons, and Vanderbilts. A graduate of St. Paul's School, Owen Wister—who wrote America's first real Western, *The Virginian: A Horseman of the Plains* (1902)—observed that Coit's recumbent marble statue in the school chapel was clothed in a monastic gown. It was an appropriate depiction, Wister thought, because the rector had been born "seven hundred years later than the days of his spiritual kin." Following the death of his wife, Mary Bowman Wheeler Coit, in 1888, Coit turned to the Cowley Fathers for spiritual solace.

Several of his erstwhile colleagues noted that after his death, his image—that of a tall priest in a long black coat—remained at the school as a kind of abiding presence.

Coit at Work

In his teaching and advising, Henry Coit had many strengths. He was knowledgeable in his subjects, well prepared and confident. His judgment of boys' character was piercing and astute. He could win over the shy lad with gentle encouragement or puncture the pretensions of the proud youth with well-chosen words. His Sunday sermons were long and laborious, but his Thursday Evening Talks, also known as Dr. Coit's Lectures, were more memorable. They dealt directly with aspects of school life, and through them the rector helped his listeners to see matters from his point of view.

Known for both his high standards and his enthusiasm, he was an inspiring teacher of Greek and Latin texts. One of his old boys, James Carter Knox (1849–1930), recalled that Coit "read aloud with manifest joy." And Knox would know: he was a student at St. Paul's from 1862 to 1867, and then organist, choir master, and English teacher there for fifty years.

But Coit also had his weaknesses in the professional realm. An absolutist, he was too certain of his judgments, which students later discovered could be mistaken. He was autocratic in administration and in his work with boys. He almost never left campus, except to visit Boston bookshops or to preach in Episcopal parishes, and so he rarely brushed up against the challenging opinions of his peers. Unused to being opposed, he grew accustomed to having his own way. His comments could be sarcastic and peremptory. He made up for his limited experience and lack of training in the teaching arts with a kind of pedagogical dogmatism.

A largely uncritical biographer, Knox slips in some telling statements: "In [Coit's] system Diligence and Duty covered pretty much all that was necessary on the boy's part." In other words, the rector viewed students as passive receptacles, not active inquirers. In turn, a teacher needed only "sound knowledge" and "the capacity to impart it." Reaching for a way to describe Coit's customary stance, Knox provides a striking image: "Dr. Coit was like a wall, if a principle was involved"— and apparently in areas beyond "principle" as well. Naturally, Knox says, "parents and masters, not to mention boys, were occasionally wounded, and sometimes alienated."

In sum, Coit possessed a "dominating manner." In class, he "would wave off any boy who ventured to cite a dictionary as counter-authority to his own translation or pronunciation." In a person "less genuine," his "moral domination" would have amounted to "a tyranny," and his "graciousness" would have struck his listeners as a "patronizing condescension."

Interestingly, Knox mentions that Thomas Arnold (1795–1842), the aforementioned headmaster of Rugby School, in Warwickshire, had a deeper sense of boys' unfinished characters—Arnold referred to "the naturally imperfect state of boyhood"—and therefore did not strive to turn his charges into complete Christians. He believed that boys "are not susceptible of Christian principles in their full development and practice."

The English headmaster meant that adolescents are by nature and experience still unformed. Time and maturity would increase their sense of themselves and of the import of Christian moral and doctrinal teachings. Boys would eventually acquire the learning and, he hoped, the sound judgment of men. The meaning of Christian truth-claims, Arnold believed, could be discerned only gradually, as individuals leaned on these principles and judged for themselves their capacitating power to make sense of the world and of their lives within it. Therefore, Arnold said he aimed only to put boys on the path to becoming "Christian men."

Henry Coit manifested no such inhibitions. "Doubtless he felt with Plato," Knox writes, "that Virtue is Knowledge and can be taught."

Balancing Coit

Coit was persistent and authoritative in declaring his school's fundamental allegiance and beliefs. He followed a sensible course in establishing his school's identity but not in seeking to influence young minds and bodies in relation to what T. S. Eliot called the "permanent things." In our mechanical analogy, he mistook what is appropriate in the outer bearing ring for what is best for the inner ring. He bore down too hard on students' natures, pronouncing apodictically on what he would have been better off discussing invitingly. On this important matter, at any rate, Arnold's understanding was sounder.

John Dewey (1859–1952) is about the last person I thought I'd turn to for wise counsel on education. But we needn't accept his entire pedagogical theory—or any of his progressive philosophy or naturalistic metaphysics—to pick up some good pointers on teaching practice. In the sixteenth century, Paracelsus knew that the dosage makes the poison (*dosis sola facit venenum*). Leaves from the beautiful foxglove plant (*Digitalis purpurea*) may be fatal if ingested, but a regulated dose and mixture can improve blood flow and help a weakened heart pump more efficiently.

John Dewey: the dosage makes the poison

Thus a dash of Dewey may be just what the doctor ordered. I join him—and many others—in seeing students as active, not passive. Confront them with a problem, stimulate their interest in the questions involved, and guide them in their reflections. In fact, learning requires a delicate balance, as the metaphor of the rolling-element bearing suggests. Church schools should be clear about which virtues are salient, and they should teach the meaning of the virtues in their full biblical, theological, and historical contexts. But in realizing the roles and applicability of the virtues, pupils cannot simply be told, *de haut en bas*, what they are and how they function. As Dewey pointed out, students should not be taught exclusively from the adult's point of view. Teaching, to be fully effective, ought to bring together the great tradition and students' passions.

Young learners must be attracted by and involved in the process of discovery and exploration, as well as in the experience of reflecting on what they've found. Where in recent events—or in days long past—have they seen virtues displayed or vices at work? Where, not only in the larger world of international relations and corporate giants but even more in their own microcosms, have they been impressed by good traits of character or disappointed to witness their opposites? Indeed, students should pay particularly close attention to what the philosopher Christina Hoff Sommers refers to as vice and virtue in everyday life. How might a better grasp of the virtues help a young person in plotting and navigating his or her own life course?

Getting Started

Almost every activity in the school day presents an occasion to sink the virtues' meanings, implications, and pertinence into the manifold tasks and interests of busy students. The best primer on this subject is Craig A. Boyd and Kevin Timpe's *The Virtues: A Very Short Introduction*. But here are some suggestions for virtue teaching, with examples:

History
Courage is a constant element in political and military history, as well as in social history—think of Martin Luther King Jr., Fannie Lou Hamer, and others. Why not raise this subject directly? Infusing virtues in the curriculum will add an intel-

lectual and moral depth to each course. Distinguish courage from both cowardice and rashness. Analyze its relationship to justice and hope. Discuss a military conflict in relation to just-war theory. When, if ever, does justice require fighting to prevent injustice to the innocent? What is the role of prudence in looking after the national interest? How does a nation avoid the sin of pride—arrogant self-righteousness—in its foreign policy? Can nations be morally selfless?

Natural Sciences

Is there room for just one class during the term that is interdisciplinary, that brings in a guest conversationalist on the topic of scientific discoveries and natural phenomena in light of the virtue of faith? What is the relation between Darwin's theory of evolution by natural selection and divine creation? Where was God in the tsunami? How is the suffering of innocent children a problem for theodicy, for comprehending natural evil in the face of an omnipotent and omnibenevolent Creator? What about moral evil? Is selfishness hardwired in our genes?

Mathematics

My training in mathematics, peaking with algebra and geometry, was so minimal and occurred so long ago that I doubted I could produce a single useful example applying any of the virtues to this field of study. Often stymied, frustrated, and bewildered in math courses, I did the best I could and was thrilled when I no longer had to take another one.

But, regardless of subject matter, isn't my student experience a common one and therefore useful to think about? Almost all students, in their assignments as scholars or athletes or artists, sometimes feel like throwing the textbook or playbook or score against a wall. Adolescents are prone to totalistic thinking, according to which a C– on one short paper may send its author into a tailspin of shame and self-doubt. So a student may need *encouragement*: a gift of courage, hope, and confidence. Teachers and coaches display any number of key virtues in such circumstances: loyalty (rooted in a kind of professional friendship), perseverance (a form of patience), prudence (perspective), realistic hope (not fantasy), temperance (self-mastery), and most of all a particular form of courage.

Courage was so vital to the ancient Romans that *virtus* came to signify not only manliness and valor but also virtue—moral excellence—itself. In its most basic form, courage means fortitude, from *fortis*, strong, brave: hanging tough, remaining sturdy. Fortitude is the virtue of a soldier who holds his ground, keeping his post against powerful opponents, like the dashing airborne commander Jumpin' Jim Gavin during the Allied invasion of Sicily in 1943. On July 11, despite his troopers' underpowered weapons, Gavin confronted the soldiers and Tiger tanks of Nazi Germany's Hermann Göring Division. Launching attack and counterattack at Biazza Ridge, he eventually prevailed "by simply refusing to give up the battlefield." That's how Gavin put it years later in his memoirs. During this bloody encounter, his words to his men were more direct: "We're staying on this ridge no matter what happens!"

It may sound ridiculous to compare anxious students who persist in Advanced Calculus, say, with parachute infantrymen of the celebrated 82nd Airborne Division in World War II. But young people today face growing challenges, including a suicide epidemic, the erosion of traditional authorities, and the morale-suppressing impact of social media. Each student has his or her unique struggles, and on some days just refusing to give up the battlefield is a victory that should be acknowledged in light of the virtues it represents.

Athletics

Outside of chapel, the field house and the playing fields are the places in a school where the virtues are most likely to be referred to on a consistent basis. A friend of mine who played football in college many years ago told me about a sign in the rafters of his university's gymnasium: "We supply the equipment; you supply the courage."

When I was in fourth grade, my football coach was Mitch Tullai, a renowned coach, athletic director, history master, and Abraham Lincoln impersonator. Coach Tullai gave me my first formal lesson in applied ethics. We had one game that year, against Baltimore's famous Calvert School, whose players we had heard were unusually big and strong and well prepared. I was excited but also a mite apprehensive.

At practice the day before the game, as if he could read our minds and hearts, Coach Tullai, a wise man, told us exactly what we needed to hear: "A courageous person is not someone who is never afraid. Courage doesn't mean not being afraid. It means overcoming your fear and doing your job anyway." What might sound trite to a nineteen-year-old is a revelation—and a relief—to a nine-year-old.

Although I did not know it at the time, Coach Tullai was talking about self-mastery as well as courage. The virtues work together. Their involution is a fascinating characteristic worth probing with students. This coinherence is especially noticeable in the theological virtues. Faith, hope, and love abide together. We can distinguish them, but in the end we cannot separate them.

Reading

This subject cuts across all the disciplines. It's a leading concern of educators today: students' limited attention spans, especially their waning ability to focus on written material of any sophistication. Adam Garfinkle has a well-researched article on this topic in *National Affairs*.

Garfinkle discusses the findings of experts in cognitive neuroscience and developmental psycholinguistics who have identified a declining capacity to engage in "deep reading," which occurs when readers interact with an extended piece of writing. They meet the author's words in a dialectical process, bringing to the text what they know and then responding to new meanings derived from the text. Deep reading of both nonfiction and novels pays huge dividends. Garfinkle notes that it nurtures abstract thought, empowers creativity, fosters imagination, generates new insights, and builds empathy.

Deep literacy has been in decline since 1949. From that year to the present day, one distraction after the next has drawn our gaze: television, the internet, the smartphone. Feedback loops reward human brains for losing focus and for repeatedly searching for new stimuli. Garfinkle comments on the dire consequences of the scattered superficiality represented by the noun *multitasking* and of reduced capacities to grasp and employ abstract reasoning. We see these consequences in realms ranging from the personal ("social autism") to the political (shallowly rooted but passionately held hyperpartisan opinions). Too often we have failed to follow General George C. Marshall's prudent advice to each graduate of the Virginia Military Institute in 1956: "Don't be a deep feeler but a poor thinker."

With weakened powers of sustained concentration, readers no longer slow down long enough to give robust consideration to a substantial essay. They lack what the neuroscientist Maryanne Wolf, in *Reader, Come Home*, calls "cognitive patience." A close relative of patience is *attention*, a word that the French

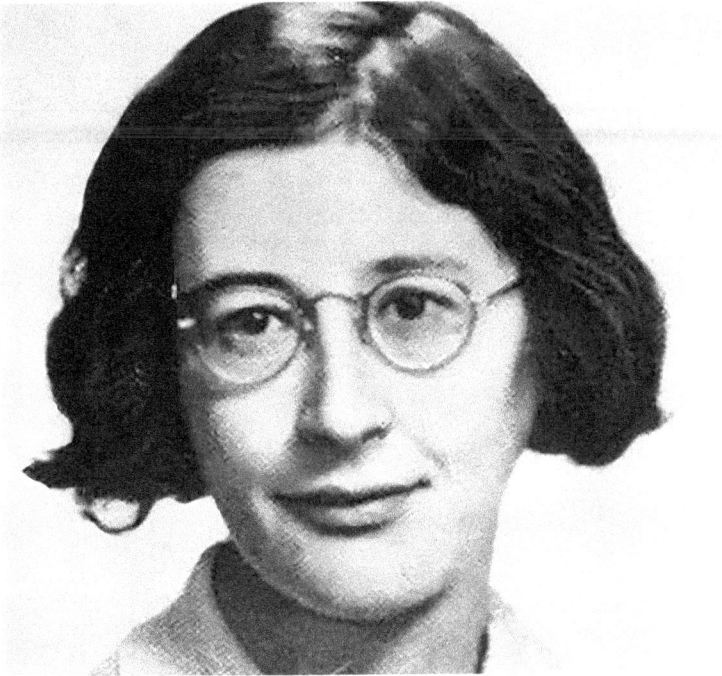

Simone Weil: teaching trains the attention

philosopher and mystic Simone Weil illuminates in her well-known essay "Attention and Will."

Weil's understanding of education is particularly relevant to traditional church schools, classical Christian schools, and homeschooling environments. She sees learning as an undertaking that invokes the ancient virtues. "Teaching," she says, "should have no aim but to prepare, by training the attention," so that students can yield full attention to the object of study. Prayer, she believes, is "attention in its pure form."

Weil's vision of participating deeply in the educative mission aligns with the "receptive ecumenism" discussed in the preceding chapter: a humble openness to receiving what others have to offer so that we might be transformed. For Weil, education has more to do with waiting than with searching. In other words, whether Weil is speaking of waiting for God, for European war refugees, for a text to disclose its meaning, or for the beauty of a work of art to penetrate our being, true attention requires patience. Patience signifies attentiveness to the initiative—receptivity to the gift—of others. It is a crucial habit for attaining knowledge and wisdom, and yet its value is not primarily instrumental.

In sum, engaging with others' challenging arguments, searching for answers in an appropriate array of sources, and formulating thoughtful responses are all proper intellectual skills that we should try to develop in our students. But Simone Weil is onto something good when she says that education solicits an attentiveness that is receptive, not intrusive and manipulative. True learning is not *au fond* utilitarian. Rather, it begins with an attitude that is more like thankfulness for a gift than a seeking after rewards.

Intellectual patience, whether manifested in active deep reading or in simple attention, is a critical virtue to have and to reinforce, both for our own good and for that of society at large. Virtues, we know, are good habits, and the word *habit* comes from the Latin *habere*, to have. Virtues are good traits to possess. But what we as a people have today we can easily lose tomorrow.

3

WRITING AS A
MORAL ACT

Like reading, writing is a subject that cuts across the curriculum—and, of course, into the world beyond school. Indeed, it's such a large and important topic that it warrants its own chapter.

I often point out to my undergraduate students that writing is a *moral* act. At first they are puzzled by this claim. Not only are they prone to compartmentalizing—discuss ethics in a philosophy class, learn writing in an English class—they are also unused to thinking ethically about ordinary, apparently nonmoral, activities. For them, morality is limited to (1) rules, such as the honor code's prohibitions against lying, cheating, and stealing; (2) social justice issues, such as the sins of the patriarchy and the faults of free enterprise; and (3) their informal sense of peer norms, such as having a friend's back during a crisis.

To expand their horizons, I invite them to think about moral aspects of everyday life and to consider the first steps of forming an ethical position and of acting morally. Sound ethical judgment begins not with prescription but with description: characterizing the situation accurately and fairly. Not "what ought we to do?" but "what is going on here?"

Limning the essential elements of a case requires sharp vision. We won't see clearly if we do not, so far as possible, accomplish a temporary "unselfing of the self," in Evelyn Underhill's phrase, attempting to perceive with others' eyes. This entire effort lies at the heart of the ethical life; it is a work of the moral imagination.

Expectations

This approach is also fundamental to the task of essay writing. The ethical underpinnings of a good piece of writing can be glimpsed even during the opening session of an introductory humanities course for undergraduates.

When I require two-page response papers, which their authors will read aloud to their peers, students at first believe I seek nothing more than a summary of an assignment's main points. No, I answer, not a bare summary. Consider your listeners; everyone would be bored to tears by a rehash of what the whole class (I state hopefully) has already read. Oh, well then, you want our opinions, right? No, I reply; no one would be interested in a college freshman's opinions; you possess no recognized authority in the subject area.

All apparent options blocked, students are puzzled and feel a trifle dismayed—but still well short of mutinous. It's the beginning of the academic year, after all, and we're just going over the syllabus, defining expectations. Now they're ready to start learning something new and valuable.

Your paper, I advise them, should be the most intellectually alert and stylistically engaging commentary on your assigned section of the reading that you can produce. Of course I shall take into account the short time frame you have at your disposal as well as your limited background in this subject. Therefore, some summary, yes—but incorporate evidence from the text in support of your thesis. Maintain command of your paper as a rider keeps control of his or her horse: subordinate summary and quotations to the development of your position.

And some opinion, yes—but opinion in the sense of your carefully weighed judgment on and compellingly argued analysis of the material. When you present your paper, your listeners will be interested not in your isolated, undefended opinion ("I really enjoyed this book, and if you like Westerns, I feel that you will too") but in your rational analysis and informed judgment. And, along the way, your fellow students will be grateful for whatever elements of wit and elegance you can deploy in your phrasing.

Most of all, keep in mind your audience, which consists of the other students in this course. Anticipate objections to your case. In your paper, respond to this imagined challenger. As you dig into your subject, consider what your readers are likely to understand. Indeed, writers cannot achieve their objectives without taking into account their readers' backgrounds. As Steven Pinker has pointed out, "The form in which thoughts occur to a writer is rarely the same as the form in which they can be absorbed by the reader."

To put these rubrics another way, this exercise is not about your personal experience and self-expression. Instead, think of your writing as being much more objective than subjective. It's about piercing to the heart of the matter and writing insightfully about this topic—for example, an image, a character, an ethical quandary, a historical dispute—supporting your case with the best logic and evidence you can muster. Steven Backus, who directed the Writing and Critical Thinking Center at the College of St. Scholastica, expresses the severity of this challenge: "Critical analysis...is a practice that requires keen observation, sharp reflection, cold-hearted logic, crisp reasoning, icy discernment, and cool evaluation."

Your paper is very much you, I tell students, representing your best self. But it is even more you in relation to your readers, as you regularly think of them and even draw your imagined respondents into the conversation. This effort to write for others, not just for yourself, is one reason that writing is not only a moral but also a strenuous activity.

Effort

I have always found that as an instructor I could enter a class tired and the teaching process would reinvigorate me. I could go into an administrative meeting spent, with no resources in reserve, but need no additional alertness to stay afloat through the proceedings. I have never been able to write well, however—to start writing, particularly—when I was worn out; the little gray cells do not fire sufficiently fast to make for complete connections between lively thoughts and their fit expression. In his essay "Why I Write," George Orwell confesses: "Writing a book is a horrible, exhausting struggle, like a long bout of some painful illness. One would never undertake such a thing if one were not driven on by some demon whom one can neither resist nor understand."

Excellent thinking and writing always entail substantial effort. If an acquaintance says that she enjoys writing, then you can be pretty certain that she's not a great writer. To paraphrase Thomas Mann, a writer is someone for whom writing is tougher, not easier, than it is for other people. I am always heartened by reports that the holograph manuscripts of lovely writers like Izaak Walton display evidence of repeated attempts to find the best wording. This additional labor is rarely in vain. It pays dividends for readers. The opposite—clumsy, somniferous sentences—is typically more noticeable than fine prose that does not draw attention to itself. As someone, though probably not Samuel Johnson, observed, "What is written without effort is in general read without pleasure."

Anyone writing for intelligent readers bears the responsibility to make his ideas intelligible. In an undergraduate course, the probability that a professor will not understand a student's written argument because it is too sophisticated is not high. The brutal reality is that students must express themselves clearly or suffer the consequences. If a paper's meaning is not apparent to the instructor, then the fault lies with the assignment's author, not with its reader.

Disappointed students will sometimes try to argue for a higher grade by launching into descriptions of what their sentences and paragraphs "really meant." Based on years of experience with dangling modifiers, missing transitions, faulty usage, and theses lacking cogent evidence, instructors can usually infer what their students were trying to say but must assess only what the students actually delivered—although they can help students see how they could have conveyed what they "really meant" in better terms.

Learning to explain complex matters well is one of writing's supreme challenges. But writing for the reader rather than for herself alone is good for an author's character; it can relax her relentless self-regard. Writers' self-absorption can affect their judgment. In *The Speechwriter*, Barton Swaim remarks that former South Carolina governor Mark Sanford, for whom Swaim worked, "knew bad writing when he saw it, except when he was the author." It's hard for authors—and especially for inexperienced writers, oblivious of *parti pris*—to appraise their work accurately.

In adopting an other-regarding stance and in laboring to engage their readers squarely, writers execute a craft that is moral in both its initiation and its accomplishment. Underscoring this point, the Cambridge scholar F. L. Lucas, in his learned and lively *Style: The Art of Writing Well*, employs a thought-provoking verb when he says that an author achieves clarity "mainly by taking trouble; and by writing to *serve* people rather than to impress them" (emphasis added).

Serve them, yes, but maintain your dignity; do not kowtow to readers. "The author of character will not bow too much to the character of his audience," Lucas writes. "Courtesy is better than deference." A courteous author keeps in mind, for example, that readers are busy people; they have other good material to read and limited time in which to read it, so strive for concision and shun obscurity. Lucas believes that Confucius hit the mark "when he said that the gentleman is courteous, but not pliable; the common man pliable, but not courteous."

Performing this balancing act—straining to express one's distinctive ideas while keeping a diverse array of readers faithfully in mind—is partly why writing is such a chore. It's one reason why good writers do not like to write; they like to have written—to paraphrase a remark attributed to the poet and critic Dorothy Parker.

Excellence

The writing process is also a moral course because it requires the habits of excellence. Two key virtues, industry and perseverance, are crucial for students to take to heart. Producing a splendid paper requires taking pains to cast one's thought in the best possible form. As William Zinsser says in his classic guide *On Writing Well*, "Rewriting is the essence of writing well: it's where the game is won or lost."

Because much of an essay's quality depends on revision, students who are bright but lazy—or fairly bright but definitely overconfident—will see their efforts go down a letter grade or two owing to procrastination. Determined to crank out papers, they fail to plan and leave little time for reviewing and revising their work. Whether felled by acedia or seduced by misplaced priorities, careless students manifestly lack prudence—and growing this capacity for practical judgment is much of what the undergraduate years are all about. Deferring gratification may require temporarily denying one's friends; thus a modicum of moral courage, too, might be needed to hold procrastination at bay.

An outstanding professional writer will take the trouble to reread her work thirty or forty times. After a paragraph is composed and revised and revised again, she might look it over and nod with tentative approval, until she begins to pick at a blemish or two and starts to work on the smoothest transition to the next paragraph. All the while, she is steadily keeping in mind the architecture of the whole essay and the (waxing or waning?) persuasiveness of her argument.

To be a superb writer, it helps to have a somewhat obsessive personality. Writing demands tremendous focus and the capacity to hold in mind many bits and pieces simultaneously.

For this reason, serious writers do not like distractions; most cannot bear interruptions. They covet solitude. Dissertation writers sometimes crash under the pressure of realizing this lonely high-wire act.

In the *Times Literary Supplement*, Brian Dillon speaks of Jenny Diski's need for peace and quiet while writing. Dillon notes how, in her book *On Trying to Keep Still*, Diski "is honest and funny on the everyday ruthlessness of the average writer, whose monstrous, adolescent need for solitude is such that Diski cannot even bear to know, when she sits down at her desk, that she has an appointment in three days' time." And yet a writer should not be so compulsive as to become a costive perfectionist. In the end, as one of my own editors assured me, a book manuscript is not so much finished as let go of.

In many cases, both children and adults put off work not because of perfectionism, overconfidence, or time constraints but rather because of anxieties about competence and control: the nagging sense that I'm just not very good at this business; it gives me no pleasure and I can envision no reward because I doubt I'll be successful. At least if I postpone completing my assignment until the last possible moment and the final result is deficient, I can tell myself I could have done better if I hadn't been so rushed. Of course, this psychological defense mechanism offers no protection at all against low marks or bad reviews.

What does provide some insurance against disaster is the virtue of hope, grounded in a realistic appraisal of one's abilities and in a prudent reliance on professional assistance. Allowing enough time to solicit advice from one's teacher will almost always yield both effective aid and healthy encouragement. Prudence counsels the struggling soul to be hopeful, to lean on the wisdom and experience of mentors, benefiting from the expertise and guidance of qualified instructors. In Part 2, we shall explore this aspect of hope in greater depth.

Success in completing scholastic requirements, including writing assignments, always requires—besides a stout measure of hope—the virtue of temperance, or self-mastery. Temperance refers to an internal action less dreary and passive than mere abstinence—renouncing parties during Lent, for example. It means disciplining oneself to realize one's greatest potential. Freedom, therefore, is the close relative of temperance. Self-mastery enables a person to be truly free: free because now equipped to meet all the challenges that life—or at least a professor or coach—throws at you.

I knew a high school football player who spent many summer hours drilling, practicing, and giving up more pleasurable activities to master kicking field goals. By the fall he had become an accomplished kicker. Now he was freer to score points for his team by kicking field goals than players—even ones with much more natural ability—who never put in the hours of practice.

Scorning self-discipline leaves a person not freer but weaker, more likely to succumb to momentary desires and transitory drives, lacking impulse control, less a master than a captive. Saint Augustine of Hippo refers to that liberty which is not true self-possession but merely its simulacrum, "the freedom of a runaway slave." Temperance is more exciting than it sounds: it stands for the discipline of the self that produces excellence and for the self-command that liberates for good.

Too often, sheer sloppiness characterizes students' essays. These papers bear the telltale marks of efforts composed in haste. Frequently, a student who reads his paper aloud in class will notice mistakes and infelicities he would have found earlier if he had engaged in this exercise prior to the class meeting.

Such discoveries are a good reason to have students read their essays aloud in front of an audience of their peers and listen in turn to their classmates' work. This practice will deepen their sense of writing to please and inform a variety of readers rather than hurriedly cobbling together a paper for the instructor—resulting in, as my father used to say, a shoemaker's job of carpentry.

Teachers do the authors of shoddy products a real disservice by awarding all papers top marks or otherwise caving in to grade inflation. Surely in these cases equity is not justice. This practice is not love, either, and it gives up on hope.

Appraisal of student papers needs to be both fair and helpful. To improve students' writing quickly, return papers at the next class meeting and then meet with each student individually soon afterward. Explain corrections, salute strengths, interpret the overall evaluation, make it clear what she has to do to earn a higher grade, and offer sincere encouragement.

Most students who receive regular advice on their writing will improve throughout the semester. Students who early on lacked confidence in their writing ability ("I'm just no good at writing") will gain both competence and increased self-assurance ("I guess I can write after all") by the last couple of weeks. It's always good for them to peak at the playoffs, as a teaching mentor told me during my first year in the classroom. Students will forget much of a course's content, but writing skills they can take with them and build on.

End

Is a piece of writing ready for release when its author has set forth a solid thesis in clear prose? Perhaps. Certainly every student I've ever taught would say yes, that's it, *finis*. But the ordinary reader would heartily disagree and beg all writers to attempt one more step: a reworking of the prose, with special attention to both problems (excessive verbiage, inadequate explanations, clunky transitions, trite expressions, awkward cadence) and possibilities (metaphors and similes, a striking phrase, a pleasing image, a little surprise, perhaps some humor).

Word choice, in particular, is an element of style that requires patience and self-discipline, as well as a good vocabulary, a sensibility both refined and demotic, and a taste for exactitude. *The Economist Style Guide* (11th edition) provides this admonition to the magazine's writers: "Words that are horrible to one writer may not be horrible to another, but if you are a writer for whom no words are horrible, you would do well to take up some other activity."

In their pithy text on ethics and leadership, *10 Virtues of Outstanding Leaders*, Al Gini and Ronald M. Green include aesthetic sensitivity as one of their ten virtues, and they associate this capacity with Apple Inc.'s Steve Jobs. A heightened awareness of aesthetics and design is a virtue not only of corporate innovators but also of the best authors. Most readers would acknowledge the merit of David Skinner's comment, in an essay in the *Washington Examiner*, that a writer might follow all the rules of English grammar and diction and incorporate no errors in his text but "still not write with any distinction." Skinner explains, "Something additional, and far more precious, is needed to achieve a style that goes beyond mere competence: an overlay of personality, intelligence, fun, imagination, verbal dexterity, the taking of positions that are somehow unique and striking, a sense of intellectual drama, ... and a great deal of effort."

Skinner's comment points to a moral habit found in exceptional writers: fortitude. Strength to take time with yourself, to persevere, and to seek the best answers and the choicest means of expressing them. Endurance enabled by a resolute character. Intellectual steeliness. Courage under adversity—or at least patient submission to the struggle that all writers speak of.

In *The Shelf*, Phyllis Rose makes a statement that I like to explore when I talk with students about writing. A writer, she says, must "fight against every sentence, resisting the pressure of convention and conformity, resisting his or her impulses toward banality and the easy way." Her arresting, quasi-metaphorical exhortation cannot be reduced to the language of direct translation. But, after we read her words, I tell students that their sentences and mine are constantly speaking back to us, saying something like "That's good enough, let it go, we're done, turn it in."

Practical wisdom might intervene at this point, ally itself with fortitude, and advise against a debilitating tug-of-war with our sentences. If we have time, we might turn off the computer for a few hours and go for a long walk or get some sleep, giving the unconscious an opportunity to resolve a knotty issue or two. Let the tangles sort themselves out if they can, and maybe better ideas will percolate through in usable form. In any event, we'll be fresher for the contest the next day.

In my own thoughts about critical thinking and good writing, I recur to Rose's injunction again and again. A writer who accepts the challenge to "fight against every sentence" embraces fortitude: being of strong heart, resisting the easy way, being courteous but not pliable, and standing firm against commonplaces of either thought or expression.

Acquainting students with the rules, goals, and methods of a vigorous, clean, clear prose style will be useful to them and to their readers. Helping students to discern the ethical aspects of writing and particularly the virtues involved in producing an effective essay might make them not only more proficient authors but also more disciplined and aware moral actors.

4

HONOR

Chapters 2 and 3 revolve around *what* is taught. They disclose ways in which common subjects can be viewed from a moral angle. Lifting a few rocks and poking at the substrate in the academic stream will reveal a host of active, lively ethical topics. Thus these chapters present ways to introduce moral questions and ethical matter not from on high but instead up close to where students are—that is, alongside the projects they are already undertaking in their ordinary academic and athletic endeavors.

Now we want to focus on *how*, for, as every math teacher knows, the way in which a problem is solved is as critical as the answer. Education is more about developing the habits—in particular, the moral traits—of a good life than it is about delivering content, as important as knowledge is. And the formation of character is, of course, where honor comes in.

More significant than grades is intellectual honesty. I always tell students that it is more important to graduate with honor than to graduate with honors. It doesn't matter whether, when honor offenders cross the stage at commencement, they're the only ones who know they've cheated; it's enough that they know. Their misconduct soils their achievement; it devalues their diploma; unacknowledged, it will hang over their heads forever.

Back to Writing

In the case of writing, we can easily perceive the crucial ways in which an author reveals her integrity in her work; we grasp how central honesty is to the final result. A conscientious writer does not dissemble. She fairly describes both her own views and those of others. F. L. Lucas says that a writer should never "write a line without considering whether it is really true, whether you have not exaggerated your statement, or its evidence." Misrepresenting a scholar by quoting inaccurately or distorting a source's meaning by paraphrasing incorrectly or omitting pertinent material is wrong, and even worse when done intentionally to support an author's thesis.

In addition, the work a writer claims to be his own should actually be by him, not by someone else. We live in an era of moral equivocation. The group is emphasized over the individual, and traditional norms are invoked as guideposts far less often than in the past. The reality of authorship appears to be up for grabs. Isn't every work the product of many hands?

Justice demands that we refuse to go along with academic deception. Plagiarism—claiming someone else's words or ideas as your own—manages to be lying, cheating, and stealing all rolled into one. Sadly, aided by the internet, it is as widespread as it is repugnant. The launch of generative artificial intelligence (AI) platforms such as ChatGPT has exacerbated the problem. I do not allow my students to receive advice from anyone else about what their papers should look like, let alone to have AI write for them. Any outside assistance I deem a violation of the honor code. The only exceptions are qualified teachers: the course instructor, tutors in the writing center, or a trusted professor, whose name students must identify on their papers.

I have three reasons for this simple rule, which I recognize goes against statements in other course syllabi as well as against the regular practice of professional writers:

First, I ask the student author, who has really earned the grade for your paper, you or your outstanding roommate—or ChatGPT? How can I award a fair grade when I don't know what you have written?

Second, if I cannot tell what specific work is yours, I cannot see where your problems lie, so how can I help you improve? The person who fixed up your prose style did not spend any time going over the fixes with you. Nor should she have; she's not qualified to do so. And the machine that wrote a paper for you won't walk through each choice of structure, style, or argument.

Third, how is employing your knowledgeable associate fair to those students who had no such assistance handy? How is relying on ChatGPT fair to those who refused to avail themselves of outside resources, preferring to rise or fall by their own efforts? This course is part of a learning process, which means gaining knowledge and getting better at essential skills of thinking and writing. Academic dishonesty is wrong in itself, and it undermines the whole point of this course, which is not to boost your GPA but to teach you something worthwhile.

Again, in school, the habits lay the foundation. They should slowly but surely coalesce to build character. Therefore, *how* a piece of work is completed is at least as important as *what* is produced.

Honor Systems

Rare is the Christian school that does not have an honor system. Typically, beginning students subscribe their names to a document attesting to their commitment to abiding by the standards of the honor code. The head of school and the dean of students can be relied on to state the code's purpose and meaning. Thenceforward, all students will have daily occasions to consider the code's requirements.

Over time, most students will take on the habits of honor. They will acquire at least an intuitive recognition of the fact that virtues and norms can dovetail. Stable dispositions of honor—including sturdy habits of self-discipline, moral courage, practical judgment, and commitment to fair play on level ground—incline students to obey prohibitions on lying, cheating, and stealing: virtue ethics and rule-deontological ethics cohering. The vast majority of students will not cheat on tests or homework assignments, they will not lie to their teachers, and they will not steal unguarded cash or jewelry from their dorm mates. Those who succumb to temptation will usually have an opportunity to shape up, or they will be severed from the community.

Beyond these familiar episodes of initial orientation and daily application, honor could be a subject ripe for examination within the school setting. But it is a golden fruit that generally remains unpicked. Rich in content, honor incorporates both moral and intellectual elements. Indeed, even the cursory examination of its form and function in the preceding paragraph revealed that "honor" is a catch-all term that comprises the cardinal virtues—what I referred to as the "sturdy habits"—of temperance, fortitude, prudence, and justice.

Probe deeper and discover connections with faith, hope, and love. In fact, the academic life, in both its macro and its micro dimensions, is largely motivated by hope. Students who commit dishonorable acts usually do so because, at least in a few fraught moments, they lack this virtue. In other words, they experience despair, which is from the Latin *de* and *sperare*, "without" and "to hope."

This loss of hope drives students to feel desperate. In their desperation, they act foolishly, rashly, even dangerously. Feeling cornered by lack of knowledge or lack of time and by the pressure of high expectations, they take chances. They fail to act with prudence, which would have helped them to set an honorable goal and to determine the right way to achieve it. Sadly, for these decisive minutes, they lack all the virtues. Prudence would have foreseen not only the amount of time required to finish their papers in good fashion but also the likely result if they plagiarized. Temperance could have held in check their wayward impulses, the tug they felt to steal a quick look at their neighbors' multiple-choice answers. And so forth. But typically the core experience is desperation, a sense of being pulled into troubled waters by the undertow of hope receding. Later, we shall look at faith and love.

A Question of Honor

To find captivating subjects beyond the usual range of superficial treatments of honor, cast a wider net. Direct pupils' gaze beyond their daily activities so students see that honor is not exclusively a juvenile pursuit, useful for keeping young learners in line. Rather, honor is also a subject worth analyzing in relation to society at large, where students will discover that dishonor lies at the root of all sorts of problems.

For example, in 2021, during and after the withdrawal of U.S. forces from Afghanistan, not a few voices could be heard asking why no high-ranking figures chose to step down or accept at least part of the blame for the botched leave-taking operation. Regardless of the underlying merits of this search for accountability, the question points to a broader reality: leading officials—from the president and the vice president down through the ranks of cabinet officers and other political appointees—are increasingly prone to slinking away from acknowledgment of serious errors. Nor do underlings any longer resign as a *point d'honneur* when they cannot in good conscience abide a policy decision.

Instead, we encounter gaslighting, moralizing, condescension, deflection, and overmastering concern to retain status and influence. Every problematic occurrence becomes an occasion for political strategizing: *Factoring in members of the press as allies or opponents, what can we say about* x *that will improve—or do least damage to—our odds of passing* y? Not straightforward truthfulness but carom-shot calculation becomes the order of the day and the operating mode of public messaging.

It's impossible to miss this ebbing of any sense of public shame, a deficiency that forestalls a sincere, full-throated admission of responsibility. And much of the legacy media is equally susceptible to this temptation of moral ease.

Even if we now see a much higher proportion of cold-blooded careerists in government and other sectors of the ruling class, this fact alone cannot account for rampant shamelessness.

Questions remain about these individuals' formation, appointment, and continuation in their posts. What was the social matrix that produced them, and what is the ethical environment that tolerates and rewards them?

Although solutions are hard to come by, the salient issue is readily apparent: it is a question of honor—or, more precisely, a set of related questions about this hoary concept. These are the deeper issues worth exploring with mature students: What is honor? Can its antinomies be resolved? Are there ways to think more usefully about honor and its pertinence to what is to all appearances an inauspicious seminary for its nurture, today's impersonal, divided, and technocratic mass society?

Problem: Ambiguity

The first difficulty with *honor* is that its meaning is ambiguous. The noun can refer to two different states of affairs—one oriented toward self-concern and investing the individual ego, the second toward self-denial and serving the larger community.

The first definition of *honor* is glory, fame, esteem; the bestowal of high regard. In his famous dictionary, Samuel Johnson includes *reputation* and *respect* as synonyms for *honor*, which he says may also refer to "privileges of rank or birth."

As Jean-Jacques Rousseau asserts in his *Second Discourse*, with its explicatory note number 15, *amour-propre*—self-love, pride, vanity—can easily turn needy, jealous, and competitive, more and more dependent on the recognition of other human beings for the self to feel not just important but also superior. *Amour-propre* goes well beyond natural self-preservation and can inspire harm of other persons. It is, says Rousseau, "the true source of honor."

Egocentric and insecure, a self-aggrandizing person needs to feel paid attention to and lifted up as worthy: a big man on campus, a top dog in business, the most virtuous resident of the neighborhood, the most powerful member of the legislature. This anxious quest for prestige can lead to misery, because comparison, as the saying goes, is the thief of joy. On the other hand, a cooler concern for acknowledgment and respect in the eyes of the wise and estimable can lead to greater virtue.

The second meaning of *honor* is integrity; possessing a clear sense of right and wrong; strong, steady adherence to principle; moral excellence. Samuel Johnson offers the following phrases in his definition: "nobility of soul" and "a scorn of meanness." *Honor* in this second sense refers to a combination of personal integrity and virtuous conduct, which, over time, builds nobility of character.

Anyone can immediately discern the distance between these two definitions of honor. In his chapter "Of Honor in the United States and in Democratic Societies," in the second volume of *Democracy in America*, Alexis de Tocqueville grapples with the "radical difference" between—in his terms—"honor" ("the glory or the shame that our fellows attach to" our actions) and "virtue" (tied to the "good and evil" that "exist apart from the blame or the praise of" human beings). A person who performs a deed according to honor, he says, acts "not with absolute good or evil in view, but in consideration of what our fellows think of it"—that is, in line with "opinion." A person who performs a deed according to virtue acts in consideration of no other motive than "the pleasure of doing it and the idea of complying with a duty"—that is, in line with "conscience." Acting virtuously requires "judgment, discernment, spiritual effort." Striving for recognition is easier: it requires only having to recall what one's peers will praise. Hence, honor needs only "memory." The "principal and almost unique goal" of honor is "to be seen and approved," which is why, Tocqueville observes, honor always has a "theatrical" character.

The incongruity between esteem and virtue is conspicuous in real life. Many renowned persons, recipients of considerable glory in their day, have lacked personal or professional integrity. Other men and women have, in the words of Ecclesiasticus 44 (KJV), perished relatively unknown, "as though they have never been," but they were "merciful," and their "righteousness hath not been forgotten." Our culture honors any number of individuals who are ethically subpar. Because of the attention these celebrities receive, young onlookers are drawn to their glow and grow up seeking to resemble them. Many upright Americans—and not only the bluestockings and fuddy-duddies among us—can see that the qualities which the crowd chooses to praise or ignore rarely overlap with what they themselves would call honorable or dishonorable. Consequently, ordinary citizens are a trifle mystified, uncertain of exactly what this word *honor* is meant to depict.

To add to the confusion, sometimes in real life the two meanings of *honor* dovetail. Consider *honor*'s third dictionary definition, female chastity, which means both conscience-guided purity and a woman's reputation for sexual abstinence (if unmarried) or for fidelity (if married).

Problem: Moral Flaws

In addition to both lexical and empirical ambiguity, a second difficulty with honor is that, even when its meaning is clear, its substance is vulnerable to attack. Not only is honor seen as redundant and expired; it is also adjudged morally flawed.

Appraised from the standpoint of universal human rights, it is deemed inferior to dignity. Weighed in the balance of Christian ethics, it is less than *agape*.

Peter Berger offers a trenchant analysis of honor in his essay "On the Obsolescence of the Concept of Honor." He describes honor as an "aristocratic concept" that was bound up with "a hierarchical view of society." The age of chivalry operated on a moral code that had varying expectations of different groups and thus attached unequal weights to their actions, "according to the principle of 'To each his due.'" This code made the transactions of everyday life relative to a person's status in society. With the rise of the bourgeoisie, "not only [was] the honor of the *Ancien Régime*" and its hierarchy "debunked"; in its place "an understanding of man and society emerged that would eventually liquidate *any* conception of honor."

This new construct, Berger writes, was "the solitary self," which modern consciousness perceives as "the bearer of human dignity and of inalienable human rights." And dignity is what modern men and women prefer: it confers status not according to rank but by virtue of one's personhood. In its light, an abandoned baby on a rubbish heap possesses a worth equal to that of a squire in his country house on the hill. Dignity adheres to the individual, no matter what his or her estate; it asserts a humanity behind the roles and customs of a particular society and its divisions.

This view is enshrined in the preamble to the Declaration of Independence and in the United Nations Universal Declaration of Human Rights. Consequently, honor's melting away has resulted not in moral decline, Berger believes, but in ethical gains, particularly for racial and religious minorities, the poor, and exploited classes. Dignity derives from a person's intrinsic humanity, apart from his or her profession, academic degrees, wealth, or family background. Moreover, dignity, freshly discovered and brought to the fore in modernity, is not a recent invention. It has an honorable lineage, with roots going back to the Bible, to Sophocles (the crux of the confrontation between Antigone and Creon), and to other texts from ancient and medieval times.

Notwithstanding dignity's merits, Berger affirms that a "rediscovery of honor" is desirable if, along the way, honor is revised. Even in the turbulent wake of the modernizing process—including the forces of technology, industrialization, bureaucracy, urbanization, increased social mobility, and pluralism—honor has a chance because human beings need institutions to provide ordered realities for themselves. And with new institutions will come, Berger believes, "a return to honor." This updated version of honor will not simply restore the mores of past cultures but will also incorporate the modern commitment to human dignity and to freely chosen institutional roles.

From a Christian perspective, as well, traditional honor is problematic. In some major respects, it bears affinities with the pluses and minuses of classical *philia*. Friendship can be a virtue, but it is selective: the love of the mutually attractive, forming a coterie that enforces exclusionary boundaries. Its in-group nature makes *philia* morally and theologically inferior to the comprehensive love of *agape*, which is love for the ungodly and the stranger, love oriented to what needs love but has not earned it (Romans 5:6, 8). Honor's embedded status within social hierarchies—Tocqueville notes that it is positively correlated with "inequality of conditions"—means that it carries a similar ethical burden.

In his notes to his chapter on honor, Tocqueville observes that of all the world's religions, Christianity most stresses the unity of humankind and the universality of its demands, based on "the general needs of humanity," not on "social state" and the customs of particular times and places. For this reason, Christians have been wary of honor as esteem: "Christian peoples have always been and will always be very constrained in using honor." Although this constraint has brought about "the weakness of Christianity" as a movement in "certain periods and among certain peoples," this universalizing attitude—recall Galatians 3:28—also accounts for Christianity's "general strength and what assures its perpetuity."

What these analyses point to is not the complete failure of honor but the need for its reconstruction. Might, for example, a system that supports honor as integrity also confer dignity on all its participants? And might not honor, like *philia* in relation to *agape*, be open to its own transformation by an inclusive set of norms and practices?

Despite problems in both the theory and the operation of honor, the notion lingers that it could have a distinctive, positive role to play in the ethical recovery so badly needed in contemporary society. Students can be challenged to ask whether this recovery is worth advancing and, if so, what form it should take.

Reconstruction

A tempting approach to the problem of honor's duplex signification is to synthesize the word's definitions into one coherent stipulative definition. Alas, this work of verbal renovation is easier imagined than accomplished. A more promising tack lies along a different course: narrative rather than proposition.

The Senff Gate, unveiled in 1916, stands at the east entrance to the Grounds of the University of Virginia.

Inscribed in marble at its apex are these words, attributed to university president Edwin A. Alderman:

ENTER

BY THIS GATEWAY

AND SEEK

THE WAY OF HONOR

THE LIGHT OF TRUTH

THE WILL TO WORK FOR MEN

As a high school senior planning to matriculate at the university the following fall, I read these lines and found them quite stirring. Quoting these words in a school publication, I included only what I took to be the heart of the matter, the three thumping iambic phrases, and omitted the buildup, "Enter by this gateway...." But now I see that my seventeen-year-old self was too impatient, for in this inscription the invitation is as crucial as the threefold discovery, the imperative as fascinating as the objects.

The University of Virginia has always stressed student accountability, so the verb *seek* was not surprising to me; it was consistent with the university's entire modus operandi. Much depends on individual endeavor, the engagement of will and conscience, going beyond scholastic aptitude.

The "way of honor" refers to the means and the stamp: the way is followed so consistently—no matter what a student's prior practice may have been—that it becomes habitual, a trait impressed deep within his or her character.

The "light of truth" refers to the core function of the university. It's a phrase encapsulating a singular purpose that's now become more controversial across higher education than anyone could have predicted forty years ago.

The "will to work for men" points to the virtues of industry and beneficence: a call to a life beyond self-aggrandizement and narrow careerism.

Accordingly, within the university, the chief object (the intramural end) is the light of truth, not the spotlight of fame or the glitter of fortune. Working on behalf of others is the larger purpose of students' training (the extramural end). And in all the strivings and achievements of both students and faculty: honor.

"Enter by this gateway" means that the student is not alone in his or her efforts but enters a community of honor, a key source and support of standards that all students are roused to live by. The Lawn, the central quadrangle that was Mr. Jefferson's original "academical village," reflects his Enlightenment ideals, particularly the fearless search for truth. The honor system, established sixteen years after the founder's death, is a call to pursue truth honestly—that is, with no tolerance for lying, cheating, or stealing by any student in the community.

Especially to a first-year student, the Lawn illuminated in the evening is an imposing sight, a correlative to the hortatory phrases on the Senff Gate. Another sort of entrance is afforded by the honor orientation. In my day, it featured all the first-year students gathered in University Hall to hear an address by a revered member of the faculty: solemn remarks delivered from a podium behind which were arrayed the student presidents of the ten schools, sitting in high-backed, red-leather armchairs.

Trust and Loyalty

The point of this little narrative is that honor is best understood as referring to an individual's living by right principles,

The Lawn at the University of Virginia

but that honor tends to draw out the finest attributes in a person when it functions within a community that has a good purpose, and preferably in a microcosm with its own distinctive places and time-honored rituals. Such an environment inspires and forms a person, in fact transforms almost everyone. It gives even those students who enter with a loose sense of right and wrong an opportunity to firm their resolve, and offers all students at least for a time the prospect of a community set apart.

The words on the gateway, the palpable reality of a noble tradition at one's feet, even the sight of the Lawn in the gloaming—all impress upon the young student that now he or she is not merely a visitor but rather a part of this entire enterprise. Love and faith may be present in this experience, too. Students may grow to love the history, reputation, and character of this place, if not all its day-to-day realities. As the object of (relative) faith-as-trust, this community of honor confers meaning and value. This side of faith is its passive aspect, reflecting the good that students receive from their membership in a select body. In response, they will enact faith's active side: loyalty to this community by way of faithful devotion to the university's standards of honor, which conduce to the well-being of all.

Thus these experiences can and typically do flow into identity in a positive way; they can spark pride, establish bonds, shape character, and summon responsibility. *Pace* Tocqueville, the two essential meanings of honor as esteem and integrity are not necessarily far distant from each other.

The right kind of pride in one's country, family, or school can pull each of us a little higher. A sense of honor can stir us to identify with and support the best that our traditions represent. It can lead us away from dishonorable acts that would discredit both the community of trust and us. Thus it reinforces an appropriate self-esteem: a respect for ourselves as moral persons, acting according to duty rather than interest or desire. In this way are honor as integrity and honor as esteem properly entangled.

A school's honor system takes into account the duality of our nature. Like the U.S. Constitution, its anthropology is Madisonian. To paraphrase Reinhold Niebuhr, human beings' capacity for justice makes democracy possible, but an individual's or a clique's tendency to abuse power once gained makes democracy necessary. An honor system represents the long-standing belief that students are good enough to make the honor code work with impressive consistency but sufficiently tempted by wrongdoing to require procedures, safeguards, and regular reminders to shore up personal dedication.

Moreover, an academic honor system reflects the interplay of individual conscience and the community's judgments of which acts are esteemed, and which are repudiated, within the microcosm of each school. Thus it comprehends both meanings of honor we have been considering. But integrity is now primary, for without moral excellence the other kind of honor is no good at all.

Honor Today

This account reduced to propositional form would assert that honor is a concept still meaningful in parts of today's society. Indeed, it is the only method that takes students seriously as moral actors. Thus it affirms the dignity of all students, who become part of the community of trust not by birth or caste but by signaling their intention to live in a manner that is higher than the rules that prevail in the surrounding culture.

Therefore honor, according to a usefully reconstructed understanding, must first of all mean excellence of character, not renown; but the customs and norms of the subculture matter, for honor is most likely to flourish in a community—a *civitas*—oriented to a good purpose. In this regard it is like all the virtues, which are good habits aiming at good ends. A cat burglar who climbs to my neighbor's fourth-story window is no coward, but his larcenous heart traduces the virtue of courage: hence no true honor among thieves.

A stipulative definition that incorporates language about this salutary relationship between individual and community is unlikely to succeed, however, because, if we start with honor's ethical meaning as a commitment to abiding by standards of right and wrong, it is impossible to say that an individual cannot be honorable apart from her community. Some heroic souls act with stellar integrity by opposing the norms of the subcultures—including scholastic ones—in which they find themselves. These profiles in honor are laudable, and they no doubt occur countless times every day.

What we can say is that the modern administrative state and political realm bear all the hallmarks of ethical weakness that commentators on bureaucracy and the managerial revolution have identified. Recent events and public responses demonstrate, however, that the concept of honor still has some life left in it and a role to play for the commonweal, on behalf of the worthy traditions and institutions of a constitutional republic.

At a minimum, honor is an ethical concept and system worth delving into much more thoroughly in high schools and colleges today. You can start by exploring honor's strong connections to both the cardinal and the theological virtues. Students will learn more not only about honor and the virtues but also about the way good communities flourish by avoiding heedless individualism and selfish opportunism. In a crazy world, the virtues offer students hope. They foster the habits necessary to resist the undertow of despair, pulling them toward lives of noisy desperation.

Part 2

VIRTUES

5

COMPLICATIONS

The aim of this chapter is not to define and explain the virtues. You can find both outstanding introductory texts and advanced studies all over the place. Rather, my purpose here is to suggest some approaches to *teaching* the virtues—some ways to engage students by turning the virtues this way and that and observing their facets from different angles.

Examining the virtues from various angles means that students will encounter complications. This chapter looks at some complications and suggests ways to discuss them with students.

Faith: Trust and Loyalty

Faith means more than *trust and loyalty*, but I've discovered that these two common nouns represent an excellent starting point. We received a taste of this definition in the previous chapter's discussion of university life and the community of honor, where these vital entities were seen as *relative* objects of trust and loyalty. Of course, *assensus* (assent to truth) is also part of faith, which assumes the reality of what a person has trust in and loyalty to.

Even though faith is one of the theological virtues, which center on God, I believe that it's best to begin an inquiry into faith not in the Creator but in the creatures. The latter lends itself to engaging discussions of idolatry, for if absolute faith is placed in what is relative, then we shall surrender too much of ourselves to that which is only finite and thereby suffer the loss of our humanity. To paraphrase Eric Voegelin, we shall be in danger of mistaking temporal realities for the eternal realm. This tragedy occurs whenever any of the finite beings—nation, race, family, social class, fame, humanity, truth, the self, whatever—usurps the place of God, who infinitely surpasses his creation in both being (metaphysical transcendence) and goodness (moral perfection).

Beginning students tend to think—or believe they are supposed to think—that anything having to do with either "faith" or "religion" is good (or bad). I've found that most students, even if they are nonbelievers, assume that they should be quiet and respectful if someone mentions subjects related to religion. You can help them to get over their delicacy and to comprehend both "faith" and "religion" as neutral terms. The realities these words point to can go either way. For example, a bête noire of Voegelin's, political gnosticism, functions as a religion; it is bane, not blessing. Communism, Nazism, and wokeism have all been identified as religions, with their own creedal statements, holy texts, moral codes, and sacred rituals.

My favorite book on faith—and a great book to teach—is

H. Richard Niebuhr's *Radical Monotheism and Western Culture*. The author defines faith as "the attitude and action of confidence in, and fidelity to, certain realities as the sources of value and the objects of loyalty." For Niebuhr, faith has both a passive side (we receive value) and an active side (we give loyalty).

Faith means conviction, an acceptance that certain fundamental things are true and that these realities can be trusted in and relied on. If faith is not absolute intellectual certainty, then at least it knows enough to have confidence that its object will return authentic meaning and constant value. And if an entity is worthy of trust, then believers will be loyal to its cause: their actions will be guided by their commitment to what they believe in. Patriots, for example, not only love their country and believe in its ideals; they also will fight for it and, if necessary, die for it.

Niebuhr distinguishes two prominent types of faith: radical monotheism and henotheism. The latter is common practice among Christians, even if we are unaware of it. Although we like to think that we are radical monotheists, single-mindedly obeying the first of the Ten Commandments, typically we do no better than to worship *mainly* one God, while secretly or openly putting our faith in other gods as well. As the Canadian-American philosopher James K. A. Smith has trenchantly observed, powerful "cultural liturgies" may exist alongside of—or even displace—the liturgies of the Church.

Consider the history of elite schools founded by Episcopal clergymen in the nineteenth century—institutions like Henry Coit's St. Paul's School, discussed in Chapter 2. Schools that initially aimed at raising up servants of the Church found themselves shepherding future denizens of Wall Street. They helped the scions of newly rich Protestant industrialists to assimilate into America's upper class and haute bourgeoisie. The "kingdom of the market," in Smith's phrase, elbows aside the kingdom of God.

Niebuhr sees henotheism as "that social faith which makes a finite society, whether cultural or religious, the object of trust as well as of loyalty." As an example, he identifies "the consistent nationalist." If a citizen's nation is his center of value, then his faith means that he will depend on this object of his confidence "not only for his own meaning but for the worth of everything else he encounters."

That's the essential meaning of absolute faith. The object of ultimate trust is, Niebuhr writes, not a devotee's "great good" but rather "the source and center of all that is good, including his own value." All other realities—truth, life, honor, family bonds—take on their significance and worth only relative to this center of value. As Niebuhr says, one valuable task of theology, which is the discipline that undertakes reasoning in faith, is to critique this situation.

The alternative to henotheism is radical monotheism, although Niebuhr believes that we in Western civilization are acquainted with this expression of faith "more as hope than as datum, more perhaps as a possibility than as an actuality." Its value-center is not a closed society but rather "the One beyond all the many, whence all the many derive their being, and by participation in which they exist." This faith relies on God as source of both being and significance. Loved along with all other creatures by God the Father Almighty, Maker of heaven and earth, the radical monotheist is in turn loyal "to all existents"—that is, to all of created being.

The God beyond the many gods may be relied on as the source of real worth: "What otherwise, in distrust and suspicion, is regarded as fate or destiny or blind will or chance is

COMPLICATIONS   79

now trusted." This trust is a response to the revelation of God in his incarnate Son. What Niebuhr refers to as the "transfer of faith" from the many gods of the social realm to the true source of being and value typically involves "a concrete meeting with Jesus Christ." In his presence, "we most often conceive, or are given that faith." Niebuhr does not reject the possibility of other paths to God, but he affirms that "this is the usual way for us."

What he means is that Christians confront in the redemptive events of Cross and Resurrection the intersection of absolute love and absolute power. This ultimate act of divine-human reconciliation—the restoration of friendship between God and humanity—is also an event of divine revelation: God is disclosed to us as—to borrow a phrase from the English theologian Austin Farrer—Love Almighty. This God, Niebuhr concludes, is the slayer of the false gods who is revealed as the life-giver. Unlike the idols of this world, this One "does not put to shame those who trust in him."

Students' interpretation of some of the virtues, especially faith and love, tends to be superficial and sentimental. They readily think of blind faith and romantic love. They see both as private affairs having little to do with the public realm. Discussions based on such work as Niebuhr's can start to disabuse them of these notions.

Considering faith raises a complication that students are bound to encounter: the dialectical aspect of the virtues.

Fath is a matter of conviction, yes. But as humans, we have a propensity to manufacture idols, and to interpose the needy, grasping *I* between the self and our object of sight. So doesn't each of us need to say both that faith trusts and that faith *doubts*?

As the theological ethicist David Harned reminds us in *Faith and Virtue*, "We can never escape the shadow of our mingled loves and loyalties to find some point of vantage that offers a detached and neutral perspective upon our own relationships." We can never see with the naked eye. Our biases, personal ties, wishes, desires, and interests are always present in our assessments of situations and in our judgments. The shadow of our egocentrism falls across all our lines of sight, making accurate vision and therefore perfect trust and loyalty impossible for us as fallen creatures.

This is a point Niebuhr suggests in his depiction of henotheism as our default faith, no matter what illusions we harbor about our own purity of heart and piety. The affirmation *faith doubts* incorporates a theologically sensible and ethically appropriate humility about ourselves: conscientious faith is ultimate trust in the transcendent One, not complete confidence in our own faith, which we ought to recognize is fallible.

Hope: Confident Expectation

The dictionary definitions of "hope" strike me as rather pallid. I propose this phrase instead: *confident expectation*. The adjective points back to faith and therefore to the involution of the virtues—another complication. Especially when considering the theological virtues, we see that they can be distinguished but not separated. Over and over again, we observe how they depend on and enrich one another. Hope is distinguished from fantasy because hope is rooted in an anticipation of the future that is both realistic and faithful.

Saint Augustine's Prayer Book, a small manual prepared by the Anglican Order of the Holy Cross, contains clear language asserting this connection between faith and hope. In a section supporting self-examination based on the seven deadly sins, it includes "distrust" under the sin of pride. A sign of failure to trust in God is a lack of confident expectation.

Beneath the tough language of this passage lies an equally strong measure of hope. Distrust means a "refusal to recognize God's wisdom, providence, and love." In other words, lack of faith leads to a failure to discern and to hold in mind God's attributes, the goodness toward us mentioned in the previous section: the ultimate Power of the cosmos now revealed not as impersonal fate or indifferent chance but as trustworthy love.

The results of our distrust are afflictions we'd be better off without: "baseless worry, anxiety, perfectionism." We cannot secure safety for ourselves by shoveling coals into the furnace of our fretting. "Timidity or cowardice in facing difficulty, suffering, or responsibility. Surrender to gloom or discouragement instead of striving for"—and here are the three traits that should replace all the symptoms of mistrust—"confidence, patience, and hope." It's a curiously affecting set of words, beating up on us while urging us—in a sense permitting us— to let go of our fears, replacing them with confidence, patience, and hope.

A priest who was anxiety-prone and too hard on himself was at the same time one of the great princes of the English pulpit: the man known to posterity as Robertson of Brighton. In one of his remarkable sermons, Frederick W. Robertson (1816–1853) preaches hope based on Christ's attitude toward past sin. In language as fresh today as it was when he proclaimed his message more than 170 years ago, Robertson tells us that "past guilt lies behind us, and is well forgotten."

His theme is remorse, and he brings to his grappling with this relentless problem—*remorse* comes from Latin words meaning "to bite again"—the attitude of Christ himself. A man is a fatalist, Robertson notes, if he looks forward to the evil he plans to commit, decides that it is inevitable, and goes ahead with his crime. But if a person looks back on the sins he's committed, seeing his sin as now "part of the history of God's universe" and not "to be wept over for ever," then he only does what "the Giver of the Gospel permits him to do."

Robertson's sermons became enormously popular when they were published after his death because they contain both keen spiritual insight and an acute awareness of human nature. He displays his psychological understanding in the wise counsel embedded in this sermon: "Bad as the results have been in the world of making light of sin, those of brooding over it too much have been worse." Remorse has done terrible harm. "It was remorse which fixed Judas in an unalterable destiny." It is remorse that "so remembers bygone faults as to paralyze the energies for doing Christ's work, for when you break a Christian's spirit, it is all over with progress." Remorse undermines hope and holds a person back from accomplishing all that he or she has been called to do. "You remember how Christ treated sin. Sin of oppression and hypocrisy indignantly, but sin of frailty—'Hath no man condemned thee?' 'No man, Lord.' 'Neither do I condemn thee, go and sin no more'" (John 8:10–11). Then Robertson's clincher, offering hope and a future: "As if He would bid us think more of what we may be than of what we have been."

The superb Anglican theologian Austin Farrer (1904–1968), briefly mentioned above, preached a sermon with a similar message. He says that God lets us fall into these errors to reveal our hearts to us. In God's mercy, he will use these occasions for our discipline—"and turn them to account in the designs of [God's] loving-kindness." We can trust that, despite our failures, God has undertaken our lives and will bring them to good. Therefore the Christian can pray: "While

Frederick W. Robertson: remorse undermines hope

we are yours, we shall never be overtaken by darkness; work out in us the purpose of your perfect will, and bring us to that day which will marry us to joy, and ring every peal in all the city of heaven."

Both Farrer and Robertson were preachers of confident expectation.

Love: Love Unites

One of my favorite books by C. S. Lewis is *The Four Loves*, an excellent treatment of its subject. As his title makes clear, "love" cannot be reduced to a short mnemonic. Nonetheless, I offer these two words as a discussion starter: *love unites.*

For more than thirty years, I taught an undergraduate course in the New Testament. Many times I had to introduce students to material they had no awareness of, such as the combination of Jewish and Platonic themes in the Letter to the Hebrews. But in the case of Paul's first letter to the Christian community in Corinth, I had to be aware of students' preconceptions.

All Christian brides—I exaggerate only slightly—choose 1 Corinthians 13 as one of the readings at their weddings. This chapter sounds very sweet, as if it was written specifically for young couples getting married: "Love is patient; love is kind.... Love never ends."

My task was to help students see Paul's letters as occasional pieces written by a missionary on the move, addressing the requirements of specific situations. Corinth was a wealthy, cosmopolitan city, a center of commerce with a heterogeneous population from all over the Mediterranean world. Corinthians were known for practicing a wide range of religious cults and for enjoying low moral standards. Paul's letter reflects the struggles and conflicts taking place in a dynamic environment at an early stage of the Christian movement within Roman imperial society.

The young followers of Christ in Corinth were not yet as advanced in the faith as many of them supposed themselves to be. Various factions had arisen, each with its own distinctive interpretation of Christianity. Some boasted that they were already perfected; they possessed the Spirit and the necessary spiritual wisdom. Believing that they were saved and that nothing could change their condition, religious fanatics proudly declared that everything was permitted; immoral practices could do them no harm. They flaunted their freedom in Christ to the point of pure licentiousness. Rivalries persisted. The church was on the verge of shattering into competing groups. Each faction claimed that only through its leader could saving knowledge be acquired. Each party's members thought only of the glorified life and forgot about the Cross. They manifested contempt for those who had other spiritual gifts. At the Lord's Supper, some stuffed themselves and got drunk, while others were left wanting.

So Paul sets out to counsel them according to his knowledge of the wisdom and love of Christ. He refuses to side with one faction over the others. He says that their boasting, their selfishness, is not the way of Christ. God reveals his wisdom not in strength and glory but in weakness and shame. Christians are free—but their freedom must be subordinated to love. Paul addresses moral questions in the community, but he is most concerned to attack the theological root of these problems. True Christianity is a willingness to recognize and accept the Cross as a manifestation of God's power. The Cross makes all this emphasis on human achievement irrelevant. True freedom means not unbridled license but freedom to love, to serve one's neighbor responsibly, seeking the good of the whole community.

The Lord's Supper should not divide the church into factions or be treated as a selfish blowout; it should be a symbol of the unity of the church. Unity should be displayed in sharing and in mutual love. Divisions are all wrong. Love *unites*. All spiritual gifts are valuable but only if they serve the entire church. Paul introduces an organic image for the community of Christian believers: "Now you are the body of Christ and individually members of it" (12:27). The members are to work together for the good of the whole body of Christ.

It is within this context that Paul comes to our well-known Chapter 13. "If I speak in the tongues of mortals and of angels"—some Corinthians had been bragging about possessing the spiritual gift of glossolalia—"but do not have love," then I am just making a lot of noise. If I "have prophetic powers, and understand all mysteries and all knowledge," but have not love, "I am nothing." Then he tells them: "Love is patient; love is kind; love is not envious or boastful or arrogant or rude. It does not insist on its own way." Therefore, "faith, hope, and love abide, these three; and the greatest of these is love" (13:1–2, 4, 13; NRSV).

Paul says to the Corinthians: "'All things are lawful,' but not all things are beneficial. 'All things are lawful,' but not all things build up" (10:23). He gives us an understanding of love that is not romantic or sentimental but instead grounded in conscience and will and displayed in action. It's also an interpretation that continues to pose questions for citizens today. We still wrestle with problems having to do with the relationship—and possible conflict—between individual freedom and our larger responsibility.

The dialectical aspect of virtues becomes especially apparent with love. Yes, love *unites*; that is our starting point. But we also know that, at crucial moments, love must let go, such as when a daughter goes off to college or a son gets married. In fact, too much constriction in a family or a relationship will twist or even destroy love. One of love's supreme gifts is the liberation of other selves to be what God intends them to be. So love unites, but also love *separates*. Ascertaining when to hold tight and when to relax an embrace is the work of the virtue that is both a moral and an intellectual faculty: prudence.

Prudence: Practical Wisdom

Prudence means *practical wisdom*. It is the capacity to exercise sound judgment in practical matters. It leads us to take into account an array of real-world conditions, including proper timing and the advice of wise associates.

In the history of American statecraft, no better example of a prudent leader exists than Abraham Lincoln. Consider his decision-making process before he issued the preliminary Emancipation Proclamation. He wisely heeded the counsel of Secretary of State William H. Seward, who backed the president's proposed executive action as a war measure but urged him not to appear desperate: *wait to issue your declaration until the Union has achieved a significant battlefield victory*. On September 17, 1862, at Sharpsburg, Maryland, near Antietam Creek, General George B. McClellan halted the Confederates' invasion of the North. It was not an unequivocal triumph—General Robert E. Lee and his army would escape across the Potomac River, and the war would continue—but it was good enough. Lincoln sent forth his historic proclamation five days later, on September 22.

Similarly, President Franklin D. Roosevelt's handling of American entry into the Second World War depended on a sound appraisal of both the popular will and the right moment to proceed. Prudence counseled patience. In the meantime, he carefully took what actions he could, moving forward with strategic planning, military preparedness, and support for the United Kingdom.

Prudence would have us consider our (and others') experiences in similar situations, the likely results of our action or inaction, our scale of priorities, our ability to meet the challenge, our capacity to adapt or change once committed, and

President Lincoln with General McClellan at Antietam, October 1862

similar factors. Prudence helps us to choose well in light of relevant conditions and in accordance with what is right and just. It links our principles with our deliberations, decisions, and actions.

In *Virtues Abounding*, his excellent and accessible study of St. Thomas Aquinas on the cardinal virtues, Mark O'Keefe, OSB, notes that "prudence is precisely the virtue that aids us in…assessing, balancing, and prioritizing" ethical norms in relation to "practical considerations in a particular situation." Prudence helps us weigh ends and means. "All of the other virtues must be guided by prudence," O'Keefe writes, and "only the prudent person can be truly just, courageous, and temperate." As indicated in Chapter 3, prudence is a virtue that's crucial not only for world leaders but also for students keeping up with their assignments, mastering their subjects, and juggling competing demands and interests.

Prudence should be the chief virtue of legislators and government officials. Regrettably, in the case of politicians, the desire for popularity—the eagerness to satisfy constituencies to secure funding and votes for the next election cycle—can thwart careful deliberation and weaken political courage. New entitlements and federal programs, for example, invariably appear much faster than entitlement reform, which remains a speck on the far horizon. Counseled by prudence and fortified by moral courage, the true statesman will bring forward necessary but possibly painful, unpopular proposals because they are both timely and right.

In his classic collection *The Politics of Prudence*, Russell Kirk wisely states that, no matter how difficult the task in a democracy, political figures should assess plans for new measures not according to criteria of popularity or "temporary advantage" but rather according to likely long-term consequences. Yet too often imprudence reigns: politicians "dash at their objectives without giving much heed to the risk of new abuses worse than the evils they hope to sweep away."

Students do not need to decide momentous questions of state today. It's enough that they take time in their classes to learn the distinctive contributions each virtue makes and to note how, within a deliberative process, the cardinal virtues work together. Political judgment should incorporate a moral reasoning that favors prudent reflection and dauntless fortitude over hasty partisanship and shameless demagogy.

A new program of the federal government, for example, looks as if it will directly benefit a certain group immediately.

But prudence recommends temperance, a bit of self-restraint, before leaping ahead: If anonymous bureaucrats in Washington take over these tasks, then what will happen to personal relations and the sense of mutual responsibility in local communities? Will the federal government handle these functions better than public servants closer to home? What will be the consequences for the intermediate institutions and traditional associations that Tocqueville admires in *Democracy in America* and Robert Nisbet writes about so insightfully in *The Quest for Community*? How will new measures affect social atomism, alienation, civil order, and personal and professional accountability?

Students ought to notice that these sorts of questions are worth taking up, not ignoring, as would happen in most schools. At least these issues will lead our pupils to see that prudence, justice, fortitude, and temperance are necessary elements in the consideration of all vital questions, public and private.

Justice: Fair Play

Justice means *fair play*. But what is fair? What do we owe to others? In *The Virtues*, Craig Boyd and Kevin Timpe acknowledge that, of the four cardinal virtues, justice "causes the most disagreement." Both "its definition" and "the scope of its application" are unclear. The other cardinal virtues focus on the individual; this one is primarily social. And that's where questions arise. Boyd and Timpe refer to disputes ranging from taxation to fair wages to freedom of expression. One could add affirmative action in university admissions, reparations for slavery, government-contract set-asides for minority-owned businesses, crime and punishment in the American justice system, and censorship and bias in the corporate media.

For teachers, questions about fairness arise every day: How should pupils from different backgrounds—such as a new girl from China—be assessed in relation to their peers? What if one student requests an exception to your policy on late papers? If you grant his request, do you then push back the deadline for everyone or just hope that the dilatory student will not tell anyone else? Prudence will come to the side of justice and help in any way it can, even as teachers strive to stay on an even keel and embody empathy, self-control, and moral courage.

In response to questions about justice, we can see, as Boyd and Timpe write, that "we have obligations to others, and the reason we have these obligations is that others have value independent of me and my interests." That's the heart of the matter. In our discussion of honor in Chapter 4, we saw that all persons—no matter their social status or extrinsic value—have dignity. Made in the image of God (*imago dei*), each human being has worth. Justice requires us to treat each person as possessing intrinsic dignity. Others' rights come with reciprocal obligations on our part.

The *virtue* of justice means that we become habituated to recognizing the dignity of each person. We become, as it were, naturally inclined toward rendering to each human being his or her due.

Debate surrounds all aspects of justice, especially when we consider "social justice." (You might ask your students what exactly the adjective adds to a virtue that is already social.)

Notwithstanding these controversies, however, the virtue of justice is fairly straightforward: based on the fact that we are children of one Father and therefore equal before God, it inclines our hearts toward playing fair.

To "all His creatures," as Lincoln affirmed, "to the whole great family of man," God grants certain inalienable rights.

In his moral assessment of slavery, Lincoln started from this theological fact. At Lewistown, Illinois, on August 17, 1858, he declared that "nothing stamped with the Divine image and likeness was sent into the world to be trodden on, and degraded, and imbruted by its fellows." In respect of justice, Lincoln's core assumption is still the best place to begin.

Courage: Steadfast Resolve

Courage represents *steadfast resolve* in the face of dangerous threats, difficult situations, or painful experiences. The most popular of the virtues, fortitude is the stuff of heroes, such as Lieutenant General James M. Gavin, encountered in Chapter 2.

Courage offers some of the clearest examples of the involution of the virtues. Faith and hope strengthen courageous resolve; love may provide its own incentives. And courage is a kind of skeleton that enables the other virtues to stand up and be relied on in the hour of need.

In *The Screwtape Letters*, C. S. Lewis has Screwtape, a senior devil in hell, offer to his advisee, a junior tempter, the following reason for why God created "a dangerous world." God made a cosmos "in which moral issues really come to the point." In such a world, human beings are provided with occasions of real challenge and with opportunities to grow into their full stature.

In the face of these trials, "courage is not simply one of the virtues, but the form of every virtue at the testing point." A soldier may be loyal to her country—until the enemy pressures her to confess to made-up crimes or to spill military secrets. "A chastity or honesty or mercy which yields to danger will be chaste or honest or merciful only on conditions." If the virtues do yield, then these traits will be revealed to be virtues lite, lacking strong backbones of steadfast resolve. "Pilate," Lewis observes, "was merciful till it became risky." In the end, he gave in to the crowd rather than put his procuratorship on the line. He acquiesced in judicial murder rather than risk troubling the fragile Roman peace.

Temperance: Self-Mastery

Temperance means *self-mastery*. In *The Virtues*, Boyd and Timpe draw an appealing connection between courage and temperance, showing how they work together for the lasting benefit of each person. The former strengthens us to take on challenges as we strive to achieve the goods established by right reason—that is, the ends that are best for us over the long haul. The latter moderates our passions and restrains our desires so that we are not seduced by pleasures—such as immoderate quantities of food and drink—that would detour us away from our good goals. John H. Garvey observes that five of the seven deadly sins represent failures in temperance: covetousness, lust, gluttony, envy, and sloth. He points out that immoderate passions present us with an ultimately frustrating detour and slow us down, both mentally and physically.

In his letter to a member of the French National Assembly (1791), Edmund Burke considers temperance and its relation to freedom. He says that if human beings cannot govern themselves, then they must submit to being ruled by others. "Men are qualified for civil liberty in exact proportion to their disposition to put moral chains upon their own appetites." If

Edmund Burke: "Men of intemperate minds cannot be free"

citizens want to live freely, then their devotion to fair play must exceed their selfish grasping. Their sober judgment must be greater than their personal vanity. They must be more willing to heed the counsels of wise and good souls than to incline their heads to the "flattery of knaves." Society requires a governor—either internal or external—on its citizens' appetites. The less self-restraint a person has, the more he or she will need to be controlled from outside.

"Men of intemperate minds cannot be free," Burke concludes. "Their passions forge their fetters." This fact is "ordained in the eternal constitution of things." And who would dispute him? His implied question is: Which form of restraint do you prefer? Civil society—people living and working side by side in a community—requires the widespread exercise of temperance for citizens to be free and fulfilled as human beings.

The Roman Catholic bishop Fulton Sheen could see that true happiness "comes from self-possession through temperance." Burke would agree. Lasting satisfaction does not come from "self-expression through license," Sheen knew. And yet in contemporary American society we observe the rise of self-expression through license—intemperance. We see the decline of community standards, self-regulation, public safety, and individual happiness. And we see governmental powers increase and become more intrusive.

Given these disruptions within our culture, discussing the seven traditional virtues will strike some as a quaint exercise, a forlorn hope, a task so unlikely to bring about any significant improvement as to make the efforts of the doomed king of Corinth rolling his boulder in Hades look worthwhile by comparison. And yet reasons to persist are discoverable. One of them is gratitude.

Other Virtues

The mention of gratitude raises another complication of the virtues: at least a dozen other virtues beyond the major seven are worth students' attention. I shall briefly mention only three, however. My general philosophy of education holds that less is more: if students graduate from high school having internalized the meanings of seven key virtues, then they will be so much better prepared for life than if they knew none—or if they enjoyed only a passing acquaintance with twenty. Taking these virtues on board means not merely going over them lightly for an upcoming test but also, in Thomas Cranmer's phrase, inwardly digesting them.

Gratitude

Ethicists typically ponder dilemmas concerning the right act to perform (or to refrain from) in a given situation. In philosophy classes, students are asked to state what they think should be done in a difficult case—such as scarcity of resources in an overcrowded lifeboat—and then to offer an account of their moral reasoning.

But another large question occurs in ethics that is less frequently discussed in philosophy courses: Why should we care about seeking and doing the good at all? What is the motivation for right conduct in the first place? This issue is well worth exploring with students. In Christian faith (but not only in Christianity), the answer is gratitude. We love each other because God first loved us (1 John 4:19).

The posthumous collection *Against the Tide* includes the poignant words of Sir Roger Scruton on this subject. In his final diary entry (December 2019), this premier conservative philosopher wrote, "Coming close to death you begin to know what life means, and what it means is gratitude."

Stability

An old virtue, now largely forgotten outside of monasticism, is stability: in his vow of stability, the monk promises to abide in this monastery or in another to which under holy obedience he has been ordered...until his last breath.

The quintessential American virtue is not stability but active instability. Everyone in the United States is striving to get ahead, Tocqueville observed; American life is a restless quest for success. This striving has resulted in many splendid achievements. But it's always a good idea to ask students to examine overlooked qualities that go against the grain. In the current climate, the virtue of stability deserves closer attention.

Patience

In *The Stature of Waiting*, the English priest W. H. Vanstone leads us to appreciate the meaning of the virtue of patience as we never have before. Central to the work of Christ and to the Christian tradition for centuries, patience as a virtue has been neglected since about 1848. The era of revolution and democratic reform in Europe made patience look more like a vice than a virtue. And, having had enough of being told to "wait," participants in the U.S. civil rights movement understandably criticized the misuse of this virtue. They raised good questions about conditions that would sanction a salutary impatience.

An investigation into this neglected virtue will reveal that we do not know it as well as we thought we did. To uncover more of its reality, we need to turn to our exemplars, starting with George Washington, for he understood not only the power of patience but also—and most importantly for the American future—the deep worth of the patience of power.

6

EXEMPLARS

Disembodied, the virtues are mere abstractions, distinguished from one another by definitions suggesting discrete cubbyholes for each good habit. As we've already seen, positive character traits may begin that way, but, once out of the starting gates, they're off and running. In real life, stable dispositions coinhere, and good qualities mix with bad.

Moreover, as Russell Kirk knew, the moral imagination, aligned with right reason, does not receive its impetus from ideas and concepts so much as from concrete images and stories derived from art, poetry, drama, sacred scripture, fiction, history, and biography. Although he gained much from the abstract reflections of such figures as Plato, Cicero, Irving Babbitt, and T. S. Eliot, Kirk recognized that, in the formation of men and women, the path to moral truth (both its discernment and its personal acceptance) more often runs through narrative than through theory. To become adhesive, precepts must ally with examples, principles with stories, virtues with exemplars.

In Edmund Burke's words, the moral imagination is that which "the heart owns, and the understanding ratifies." It acknowledges both the fact of human sinfulness and the reality of human dignity. Therefore, as Kirk writes, the moral imagination "aspires to the apprehending of right order in the soul and right order in the commonwealth." A moral imagination that has no room in its stock of images for the welfare of the larger community would be a counterfeit, a treasure chest of private fantasy or malign mischief. Thus the liberty of the moral imagination is real freedom—the most expansive kind of freedom—because ordered by true authority.

George Washington (1732–1799): Patient Power

In 2020 a group demanded the removal of George Washington's statue from the campus of the University of Washington. Another outfit called for displacing, renaming, or "recontextualizing" the Washington Monument, the eighty-thousand-ton obelisk on the Mall of the nation's capital. A crowd of protesters in Portland, Oregon, lit a fire on the head of a statue of Washington before pulling it to the ground. Spray-painted on this figure were such words as "Genocidal Colonist," "You're on native lands," "BLM," "1619," and "Big Floyd." Some observers have wondered whether the name of Washington & Lee University will eventually be reduced to an ampersand.

We see in this focus on George Washington's sins of omission and commission a growing tendency to embrace Mark Antony's lines from William Shakespeare's *Julius Caesar*:

Smithsonian American Art Museum

George Washington: duty over desire

The evil that men do lives after them;
The good is oft interred with their bones… (III.2)

By no means are all the criticisms of Washington without
merit. Both scholars and journalists have thoroughly analyzed
Washington's opinions and practices as a slaveholder, which
reflected his rank injustice toward his fellow human beings.
Readers of biographies and visitors to museums have benefited from balanced historical assessments of the Founders'
lives, including Washington's. For Christians in particular—
believers in the doctrine of original sin—demythologization
can hold few surprises.

Notwithstanding his flaws, I continue to revere George Washington, and I rank him first among our former presidents. About the virtues in particular, he still has much to teach us. He embodied patience, temperance, courage, a sense of duty, and honor.

The ancient Christian virtue of patience might not be the first trait we associate with Washington, who employed power as an aggressive commander, a fighting revolutionary. But this moral habit is a key to his success as both soldier and statesman. In his professional career, we perceive the effectiveness of all three forms of patience: waiting, perseverance, and relinquishment.

Writing in the *Oxford Companion to Military History*, Hugh Bicheno highlights the impact of patience on the course of the American Revolution: "With [British general Henry] Clinton bottled up in New York, it was [Washington's] patience that brought the war to a successful conclusion." Washington displayed patience with the French, who were slow in coming to the Americans' aid; patience with mutinous Continental Army officers; patience with a Congress that demanded results but did not provide resources in a timely manner; patience while American general Nathanael Greene lost battles in the South but ultimately prevailed. In short, he waited for the right coalition of forces to come together at the right moment.

At least as crucial to American victory was waiting's close companion in the school of virtue: perseverance. During the winter of 1777–1778 at Valley Forge, men froze and starved to death before their commander's eyes. Typhus, pneumonia, and dysentery ran through the camp. From Valley Forge, Washington wrote of soldiers without clothes, blankets, or shoes. His officers went home on furlough; Washington stayed in camp with his men. He persevered in the face of crippling supply and money problems, second-guessing by Congress, and military setbacks. In a letter to George Clinton, governor of New York, written on February 16, 1778, he praised "the incomparable patience and fidelity of the soldiery."

Fighting on behalf of an honorable cause—as in the case of civil rights—may seem impatient. But perseverance in a worthy undertaking may be one of the highest expressions of patience, where patience means being responsive to citizens' just claims and a willingness to go to the limit on behalf of what is right. In precisely this respect was the complaining, apparently impatient Job truly patient: he insisted on justice, declared what was right (as God acknowledges in Job 42:7), and persisted in his cause.

Josef Pieper, in *The Four Cardinal Virtues*, declares that patience does not mean "an indiscriminate, self-immolating, crabbed, joyless, and spineless submission to whatever evil is met with." Quite the contrary: patience enables a person not to be defeated by evil, not to be bowed down forever by sorrow and grief. It certainly does not mean capitulating to the way things happen to be and surrendering to a terrible status quo. "Patience does not imply the exclusion of energetic, forceful activity," Pieper makes clear. Rather, patience "keeps man from the danger that his spirit may be broken by grief and lose its greatness."

A third meaning of "patience" is especially intriguing in its relation to power: handing over. W. H. Vanstone emphasizes this feature of patience in his spiritual classic *The Stature of Waiting*. Washington surrendered power, resigning as commander in chief of the Continental Army on December 23, 1783. This act astonished many because it was so unusual: everyone knew that great victors' thirst for power was unquenchable.

Mindful of the glaring exception of slaveholding, we can still affirm that Washington understood that relinquishment is a prerequisite of freedom.

How did he learn patience? Historians provide several answers. Certainly his response to the patriot cause effected modifications in his conceptions of honor, power, and patience. The larger cause of liberty reduced his assessment of the worth of possessing authority not granted by the people. His republican turn also influenced his understanding of slavery. Before the Revolution, he shared the attitudes of other Virginia planters of his day and did not question the morality of slave ownership. After the Revolution, having been exposed not only to liberal rhetoric about the rights of man but also to the opinions of young abolitionist officers whom he respected, he came to view the institution with repugnance, expressing his desire for an end to the slave trade and for gradual emancipation. And he cared about how posterity would view him. In this new nation, his honor—his reputation for integrity—depended in part on a transformed interpretation of the rights of enslaved persons.

Attending to the demands of this nascent republic, with its new political realities, required patience in all its forms. And in a republic, leaders must accommodate themselves to what the Danish philosopher Søren Kierkegaard, in *Purity of Heart*, refers to as "the slowness of the Good." Representative government frequently requires tremendous patience.

For George Washington, his stature and his standing down were two sides of the same coin of character and command. He achieved nobility in the way he patiently responded to the initiatives—and the yearnings—of his countrymen.

A sometimes rash young officer, Washington knew that to realize his goals, he had to restrain his impetuous nature. He could not let his fiery temperament, his occasional recklessness, take root in his will. Like the Englishman Samuel Johnson, he had to reject the notion that humans are perforce governed by a "ruling passion" they cannot control. Washington learned self-mastery. The virtue of temperance helped make him an outstanding commander. By controlling his ego, he was able to let go, thereby enabling his fellow citizens to flourish.

Washington was an immensely brave man. Biographer Richard Brookhiser states that at Yorktown in 1781, as Washington was inspecting the field of battle, one of his aides expressed concern that the commander in chief was too exposed to the enemy's fire: "Had you not better step a little back?" Washington replied, "Colonel Cobb, if you are afraid, you have liberty to step back." Brookhiser and fellow biographer Ron Chernow see bravery, too, in Washington's decision in his will—probably over the objections of his legatees—to go beyond what most of his peers were willing to do and to free all his slaves following the death of his wife, Martha.

In George Washington we discern, as well, a devotion to duty over interest or desire. After the Revolution, the commander of the Continental Army sought only to retire to Mount Vernon, there to enjoy his estate "under his own vine and fig tree." But his leadership abilities and his manifest trustworthiness, demonstrated in his refusal to seek a crown, made him everyone's first choice to head the new federal government. Washington truly did not want the job. He "had seen fit," historian Joseph Ellis writes, "to apprise all who inquired that he was permanently embedded...at Mount Vernon and had no intention to budge."

The only reason that Washington agreed to become the first president was his overwhelming sense of duty. "In effect," Ellis writes, "once he stepped back onto the public stage in

Philadelphia, he had committed himself, and there was now no way he could avoid leading the launch." That was Alexander Hamilton's argument at any rate, to which Washington could reply only that he was overwhelmed by "a kind of gloom." Accepting the presidency "would be attended," he said, "with more diffidence and reluctance than ever I experienced before in my life." He was not being coy. Ellis comments, "No president in American history wanted to be president less than Washington."

Duty is an unnatural virtue. We are not naturally inclined to perform it. We carry it out for the sole reason that it is the right thing to do. Having a strong sense of duty is a virtue. It goes with certain professions, the military especially. Like all the virtues, it cannot be viewed in isolation. Duty to country should not be carried out if we would thereby participate in a great evil, such as genocide. Duty is subservient to and must be assessed in light of our allegiances. Which means that our faith—what we trust in for true meaning and lasting value—determines our loyalties and hence our duties.

The new republic was not the ultimate object of Washington's faith, but, under God, the United States was worthy of his unstinting service and sacrifice. Writing in the *New Criterion*, Daniel Johnson indicates what is at stake if this service is avoided. Johnson writes that duty "is the civic virtue *par excellence*" and that "its dereliction . . . is fatal to [the] republic."

George Washington's sense of honor is well known. He embodied both meanings of honor—esteem and integrity. Having given the concept considerable thought, he frequently employed the word *honor* in his writings, and he unquestionably cared about others' regard for him. He was ever eager to maintain and to augment his reputation in the eyes of his countrymen.

But honor-as-virtue occupied a higher place in his estimation than honor-as-glory. In *Washington's Revolution: The Making of America's First Leader,* Professor Robert Middlekauff says that Washington cared about more than his standing among his peers or within the public at large. His inner being—incorporating, as we have seen, a powerful sense of duty—had to conform to virtue's requirements. A base motive would be doing what is right only to win plaudits for his efforts. To Washington, honor resided deeper in his nature than mere fame or others' regard for his virtue. Honor also signified and summoned, Middlekauff notes, "attachment to truth, honesty, and responsibility to others." As Washington's character formed, his personal strength increased, resulting in "a disposition to hold to his certainties, all summed up in a profound sense of 'honour.'" Washington's character took shape through his commitment to virtue and in the helpful context of a community that appreciated what he stood for as a principled leader.

George Washington's example stands firm. With the assistance of excellent biographical treatments—such as the studies by Gordon S. Wood, Myron Magnet, Brookhiser, Chernow, and Middlekauff—you and your students can observe the struggles he faced and the challenges he met.

Study both his vices and his virtues. Grapple with the actuality of a consummate leader who was limited in his moral vision and therefore unjust in his treatment of many of his fellow human beings, but also courageous and patient, responsive to the claims of duty and honor. Consider the complete Washington: not a marble man or, even worse, an impassive, two-dimensional cutout, but the real deal, manifestly imperfect but exemplary in crucial respects.

Hannah More (1745–1833): Moral Imagination

For all of us, some practices come more easily than others. Among Hannah More's talents was her ability to offer counsel on good and bad habits. Her wide experience gave her an opportunity to observe all sorts of human beings in all classes of society. As an educator and a writer, she knew how to nurture the self-awareness to recognize weak spots and the courage to address them and move forward. Especially perceptive are her frank comments on a problem George Washington had to confront: a virtue necessary but not native.

In *Practical Piety* (1811), More advises that if we want to improve, then "we should cultivate most assiduously, because the work is so difficult, those graces which are most opposite to our natural temper." The strength "of our good qualities," she points out, depends "on their being produced by the victory over some natural wrong propensity." More sees that "the implantation of a virtue is the eradication of a vice." Thus, she acutely observes, "it will cost one man more to keep down a rising passion than to do a brilliant deed." Another person will have more trouble holding "back a sparkling but corrupt thought" than giving "a large sum in charity."

Why? Because in the case of this last fellow, for whatever reason in his formation, generosity is a natural virtue, whereas patience—which bids him wait and attend to the words of others instead of horning in with his own clever, cutting comments—is an unnatural virtue. This person must work hard to develop forbearance, chiefly by checking his thrusting ego.

To discover fascinating case studies of this phenomenon, most of us need venture no farther afield than our own family histories. My mother—by nature or nurture, by choice or calling—was patient to the point of saintliness. My father was

Hannah More: the embodiment of ordered liberty

congenitally impatient, habitually hyperkinetic—save when his sons needed him most, and then all his peripheral projects came to a standstill.

An educator, a playwright, a novelist, a poet, an abolitionist, a philanthropist, and a spiritual writer, Hannah More was an evangelical Anglican who lived and taught the virtues, faith preeminent among them. In her *Christian Morals* (1813), for example, may be found her words on submission to divine authority. She criticizes a type of fortitude that is rooted not in Christian faith but in selfish pride: "There is a haughty spirit which, though it will not complain, does not care to submit." It proudly endures affliction and stubbornly refuses to grumble, and all the while it embraces not the will of God but "the scorn of pusillanimity." Thus "the mind puts in a claim for a merit to which the nerves could make out a better title."

"True resignation" is something different. It can be learned not from "the wise sayings of the ancient philosophers" but only from "the Great Teacher." In praying the Lord's Prayer and saying, "Thy will be done," we may offer to give up what we would most like to hold on to. To help us, God gives us "incentives to humility." He knows that self-will and felicity oppose each other; "pride and peace are irreconcilable." Faith means trust in the will of God and is the opposite of sinful pride. Both pride and faith can present fortitude, but only one stance secures peace.

More was wise about the virtues and the significance of habit. *Practical Piety* offers insights into the vanity that lies at the foundation of almost all our sins. Her concern has to do with our mixed motives. In doing good, we may opt for the grand gesture that will gain attention, while we "overlook the hourly occasions which occur of serving, of obliging, of comforting those around us."

For example, some wealthy individuals perform acts of attention-grabbing munificence. But "the habit" displayed in responding to countless small needs out of the public eye is a better reflection of "the disposition and bent of the mind than the solitary act of splendor." For support, she quotes St. Paul: "The Apostle does not say whatsoever great things you do, but 'whatsoever things ye do, do *all* to the glory of God'" (1 Cor. 10:31).

Faith infused More's life and work. Love and hope she offered regularly, within "the hourly occasions." She made the most of her opportunities, and she did not wait for the perfect constellation of circumstances to act.

Someone only vaguely familiar with More's story might mentally dismiss her as a paragon of feminine constraint, supercharged religiosity, and bluestocking pedantry. These elements are certainly present in her life and work. But a larger acquaintance will lead the observer to marvel at the range of More's accomplishments and at the freedom of her spirit.

Once she had internalized a few principles, which could be boiled down to the Summary of the Law (Matt. 22:37–39), and incorporated key virtues (courage, perseverance, piety, hope, humility, and generosity, among them), she apparently felt, in some profound sense, remarkably free. This liberty was not postmodern antinomianism but a centered, practical freedom to love.

Contemporary attitudes inhibited More. For example, opponents of the schools she started, hidebound local landowners in particular, would not allow her impoverished students to learn to write. They did not want to give these wretched children ideas above their stations in life. A More-appointed schoolmistress could lead children in reciting the Lord's Prayer or in repeating collects from the prayer book of the Established Church, but no end of trouble would ensue if she allowed any extemporaneous, "Methodistical" praying. And More herself declined an invitation to become an honorary member of the Royal Society of Literature, believing, in her words, that "I have no claim to it, [and] I consider the circumstance of sex alone a disqualification."

Yet: intelligent, gifted, winsome, original, and—in the public sphere—distinctly assertive, she prevailed. She talked and ate with whomever she wished. She went wherever she wanted to go.

More entreated her students to examine their lives and to consider how to apply the lessons they had learned. In teaching middle-class girls, she aimed to enable them to become more than mere "ornaments," capable only of making witty comments and of amusing others through their playing and singing. In her book *Strictures on the Modern System of Female Education* (1799), she says she hopes that women "will not content themselves with polishing, when they are able to reform; with entertaining, when they may awaken; and with captivating for a day, when they may bring into action powers" whose effects will last for eternity. More wanted to see young women grow into morally and intellectually capable persons, well furnished with ideas and principles, habits and qualities, to support upright, coherent lives.

More was often in poor health, suffering from debilitating headaches and chest colds and other afflictions. But she persisted—and achieved stunning results.

Born at Fishponds, just east of Bristol, England, Hannah was the fourth of five daughters of Jacob More, a schoolmaster, and his wife, Mary. In 1758 Jacob established a girls' school in Bristol. First attending this school at age thirteen as a pupil, Hannah became a teacher there at sixteen. By this time, she had studied Latin, Greek and Roman history, mathematics, French, and of course the fundamental Christian texts: the Bible and the *Book of Common Prayer* foremost among them.

Although as a teacher More required much memorization, she also made full use of her charges' imaginative powers, bringing to life characters from the Bible and from children's stories. In her pedagogy, she sought to engage her pupils' affections as well as their minds. She made routine lessons dynamic rather than dull, providing her girls with images that would last.

For example, she wrote a series of sacred dramas for the instruction and edification of her Bristol students, who acted in these plays. When she published the dramas in 1782, some laypeople and clergymen objected to her putting biblical characters on the live stage. But clearly what she was doing would have pleased Russell Kirk, who understood that the moral imagination benefits from such efforts.

In *Strictures*, she counsels teachers of religion, in particular, to avoid dry lectures and instead "interest [pupils'] feelings." Introduce "lively images." Relate, "by a warm practical application," what children have learned "to their own hearts and circumstances." Too many teachers, she says, make lessons in Christianity "uninviting." Instead, employ "the most entertaining powers of the human mind." Do not rely on rote learning. Use examples, "animated conversation," and "lively discussion." Look to Jesus himself as a model for effective teaching: introduce "interesting parables," for they not only correct character and guide understanding; they also leave room for students to "exercise" their own "ingenuity" in finding "the solution." Follow Jesus's example: seize on "surrounding objects, passing events, local circumstances, peculiar characters, apt allusions, just analogy, appropriate illustration." To assist in teaching, "call in all creation, animate and inanimate." Use "incidental imagery" to capture the imagination.

In 1774, accompanied by two of her sisters, More traveled to London and, in May of that year, met the actor-manager David Garrick for the first time. She soon became close friends with him and his wife, Eva, and through them she became acquainted with Samuel Johnson, Sir Joshua Reynolds, Richard Sheridan, Edmund Burke, the bluestockings Elizabeth Montagu and Elizabeth Carter, and Edward Gibbon. With the support of David Garrick, her first play, *The Inflexible Captive*, was performed at the Theatre Royal in Bath in April 1775. Garrick produced her next play, *Percy: A Tragedy*, which proved a splendid success when staged at Covent Garden, London, in December 1777.

In 1787, More became friends with William Wilberforce, philanthropist, member of Parliament, and famous opponent of the slave trade, and with John Newton, abolitionist and writer of hymns (including "Amazing Grace" and "Glorious Things of Thee Are Spoken"). Newton, Karen Swallow Prior reports in her biography of More titled *Fierce Convictions* (2014), deepened her evangelicalism and turned her commitments toward education and reform throughout English society. More played a significant role in the antislavery movement in Britain, where the slave trade was abolished in 1807 and slavery finally ended in 1834. Prior calls her "the single most influential woman in the British abolitionist movement."

More's widely read poem "Slavery" was published in 1788, when the slave trade was at full flood. Her condemnation of this vile practice was rooted in her Christian faith and in her understanding of human beings' shared humanity. In this poem she entreats that "Faith and Freedom" might "spring from Britain's hands." And she addresses the God who made all creatures:

> And Thou! great source of Nature and of Grace,
> Who of one blood didst form the human race;
> Look down in mercy in thy chosen time...

In answer to Wilberforce's urgent prompting, she and her cherished sister Patty in 1789 began to establish Sunday schools—education for indigent children, not classes after Sunday-morning worship. Teaching occurred on Sundays because the Sabbath was the only day that many children had available for learning.

The More sisters' Sunday schools combined religious training (the Bible and the Catechism) with lessons in practical skills, such as knitting and spinning, suitable for the children's employment as servants. Hannah and Patty More also established friendly societies—organizations for insurance and mutual assistance—and other philanthropic organizations to aid adults.

By 1790 Hannah More had formed a clear impression of the French Revolution: "I have conceived an utter aversion to liberty according to the present idea of it in France. What a cruel people they are!" She thought highly of Burke's *Reflections on the Revolution in France*, affirming that his book contained the "deepest political sagacity."

In February 1792, the second part of Thomas Paine's *The Rights of Man* appeared; it was its author's answer to Burke. More's longtime friend Beilby Porteus, the bishop of London—an evangelical and a leading abolitionist—exhorted her to produce a work aimed at the poor, who, in large numbers, were imbibing Paine.

In response to Paine, she wrote an imaginative story, published in an inexpensive pamphlet called *Village Politics* (1792), which was "addressed to all the Mechanics, Journeymen and Day Labourers in Great Britain." This story consists of a dialogue between Jack Anvil, a blacksmith, and Tom Hod, a mason. The latter has been reading *The Rights of Man*, an experience that has made him "very miserable." He longs for liberty, equality, and a new constitution. In response to Tom's demand for "reform," Jack tells him that "the shortest way is to mend thyself." Asking for "a *general reform*," Tom is met with Jack's advice: "Then let every one mend one."

Jack tells Tom that French freedom means "there's nobody safe," for they rob and kill "whom they will." The English, he reminds Tom, enjoy equality "under the law." "But have you read *The Rights of Man?*" Tom asks Jack, who answers: "No, not I, I had rather...read the *Whole Duty of Man*," referring to a High Church devotional work published in 1658. When Tom says he seeks a "perfect government," Jack tells him there's no such thing. The French brag about having liberty of conscience and of the press but in reality have neither. Their equality amounts to the right of "every man to pull down every one that is above him, till they're all as low as the lowest." And although they speak of "enlightenment," in practice they encourage citizens "to put out the light of the gospel, confound right and wrong, and grope about in pitch darkness." After Tom acknowledges that "we're better off as we are," Jack points out that no government "can make a bad man good or a discontented man happy."

More declared her pamphlet "as vulgar as heart could wish," but her demotic approach made her ideas accessible without undermining the value of her insights. Well received, *Village Politics* achieved high sales and was widely circulated.

In the summer of 1794, Paine published *The Age of Reason*, a deistic assault on biblical faith. Between 1795 and 1798, More, her sisters, and several other contributors responded with short pieces later collected under the title *Cheap Repository Tracts*. More contributed about 50 of the 114 that were published, and she served as editor for all of them. These tales and ballads took up various moral, theological, and political subjects. More employed a down-to-earth style, encouraging, by means of examples to imitate and accounts of disastrous outcomes to avoid, such virtues as sobriety, self-reliance, patriotism, humility, and industry. The tracts sold 300,000 copies in their first six weeks and more than two million copies by March 1796.

Over the following years, More published her only novel, *Coelebs in Search of a Wife* (1809), which combined a romantic plot and sturdy morals. It turned out to be her best-selling piece of writing. In her last decades, she penned books of spiritual counsel, including *Practical Piety* and *Christian Morals*.

More still fascinates us because she was at the same time traditional—respectful of civilized customs and of the moral law, scornful of self-indulgence and of unrestrained desires—and bold. In her excellent biography of More, subtitled *The First Victorian*, Anne Stott writes: "The woman who, in her youth, had seen fit to quote Pericles and urge women to shun public life was in her old age an ardent supporter of female activism, provided it kept within the bounds of modesty—though even here she could be surprisingly flexible." An orthodox Christian and personally humble, More embodied ordered liberty. Believing in the permanence of human nature, she understood that freedom is best used when guided by biblical teaching and balanced by a strong sense of responsibility.

More could maintain the principles of order and liberty in healthy tension with each other because she had deep faith and—as Stott suggests—a dollop of blissful inconsistency. *Mendip Annals* (1859), Patty More's published journal describing her and her sister's work on behalf of the education of the poor, makes it clear that the sisters simultaneously preached acceptance of one's lot in life and fostered social betterment. They instructed the poor to "do your duty in that state of life where God has placed and called you." And they cautioned against rebellion, pointing out what it had led to in France. But Patty More's account also speaks of how the two women contended with a highhanded landowner who harrumphed that he did not want these ladies coming "to make his ploughmen wiser than himself." His illiterate wife insisted that "the lower class were fated to be poor, and ignorant, and wicked," and we cannot "alter what was *decreed*." Hannah More intervened nonetheless, pulling indigent children up from ignorance and occasionally raising the social position of a worthy candidate.

One young collier in this mining district was maimed when the pit fell in on him. More determined that he had "too good talents to be sent back to the pit, the damps of which...threatened him with insanity." So she enabled him to study at "a good school, to add writing and arithmetic to his religious knowledge." The coal miner eventually became a schoolmaster.

Hannah More was a conservative but no reactionary. She made the most of her vital moral imagination and worked to quicken the moral imaginations of others, both rich and poor.

Booker T. Washington (1856–1915): Prudent Reform

Some students who pursue higher learning are more motivated than others. Among the undergraduate students I've known, some have had a drive to be the best, but a surprisingly large number have not. Aspiration is a positive character trait, especially if a person's goals transcend individual prominence or credentials for a new post and include magnanimity: an ancient virtue that stands for nobility of soul, greatness of mind and heart, generosity rather than meanness.

Booker T. Washington had this determination to excel—not only for himself but also on behalf of millions of others. He began with almost nothing except for his personal capital: his intelligence, character, and resolve. As he says in the first sentences of his best-selling 1901 autobiography, *Up*

Booker T. Washington: prudence and foresight

from Slavery, he was "born a slave on a plantation" in Franklin County, Virginia, and did not know the exact date of his birth. His father was a white man who never contributed to his rearing or even acknowledged him, and his mother was an enslaved African American woman. To the latter, Jane, goes the credit for instilling in Booker the essential virtues of honesty and industry.

The young Booker knew no occasions of play; he was not aware of having any last name. As an enslaved child, he could only carry his young mistress's books to her schoolhouse door and watch the white children engaged in study within. This sight captured his imagination: "I had the feeling that to get into a schoolhouse and study in this way would be about the same as getting into paradise." From early childhood, he'd experienced "an intense longing to learn to read." His mother, who was illiterate, did everything she could to help him find the means of doing so.

Following emancipation, Booker moved with his mother and brother to West Virginia. During the day, he worked hard, first in a salt furnace and later in a coal mine. In the evenings, he attended a school for former slaves, both children and adults. Called on to state his name, he immediately gave himself his surname, choosing, as he later said, "the best name" he could think of.

Booker Washington aspired to more than the limited prospects offered by his region's coal mines, for he'd noticed that the young boys who worked as miners had little chance of advancement. They often became "physically and mentally dwarfed," he wrote. "They soon [lost] ambition to do anything else than to continue as a coal-miner."

At this point in his life, stability would not have been a virtue; prudence counseled movement. In 1872, at age sixteen, he traveled about four hundred miles, walking much of the way after his money ran out, to the Hampton Normal and Agricultural Institute, in Hampton, Virginia, which had been founded in 1868 for freedmen and their descendants. He arrived at the institute hungry and dirty and nearly broke, but he prevailed upon its administrators to give him a chance. From the start, his experience at Hampton was transformative. His "new world" incorporated practices he'd had no experience of: eating at regular times, using a bathtub and a toothbrush, and sleeping on bedsheets.

One of the chief benefits he derived from the institute, he recalled, was apprehending the point of education. Like many people, he'd supposed that "to secure an education meant to have a good, easy time, free from all necessity for manual labour." But at Hampton he came to construe the habit of industry in a new light: "it was not a disgrace to labour." He found meaning in work, appreciating it for its financial reward but even more for its own sake, as well as "for the independence and self-relance which the ability to do something which the world wants done brings."

He learned, also, to value "unselfishness," discovering that "the happiest individuals are those who do the most to make others useful and happy." These elements would compose the heart of Washington's educational creed going forward. His salient virtues were prudence, justice, courage, hope, perseverance, and industry.

After graduating from Hampton and teaching at a school in West Virginia, Booker Washington in 1881, at age twenty-five, was appointed the principal of a new school for African Americans in Tuskegee, Alabama: the Tuskegee Normal and Industrial Institute (now Tuskegee University). When he arrived, the school had no land, buildings, or equipment. The state legislature provided a meager $2,000 in annual appropriation. He went through the surrounding area recruiting a student body composed of poor African Americans, who then built the campus.

From this point on, stability became a virtue to be held close. Although Washington traveled for months every year to raise funds, he never sought another permanent home. He was soon identified with this academic enterprise in a way that was good for it and good for him. He served as head of the Tuskegee Institute until his death there on November 14, 1915. From his base at Tuskegee, Washington became both renowned and esteemed: the primary spokesman for blacks in America.

Theodore Roosevelt sought him out as an adviser and, on October 16, 1901, hosted him at the White House for dinner with his family. This event, held at a time when the Jim Crow mindset was at its most virulent, was widely condemned by white politicians and newspapers throughout the South. One notorious political figure was the future governor of Mississippi James K. Vardaman (1861–1930), a left-wing populist and white supremacist, who declared that as a result of Washington's visit, the White House was now "so saturated with the odor of the n—— that the rats have taken refuge in the stable."

Four years later, on October 24, 1905, Roosevelt visited the Tuskegee Institute as part of a political swing through the South. By this time, twenty-four years after its founding, the school had thirty-four buildings. In his speech there, the president remarked on the school's emphasis on building character: "It is because Tuskegee stands for the moral, as well as the mental and physical, sides of training that I will do all I can to help."

Biographer Robert J. Norrell notes that by the 1960s, Tuskegee whites cherished a rosy picture of race relations during Washington's time, glossing over how frightening and deadly those years actually were. When President Roosevelt visited, "threats against the life of Booker Washington had been pouring into Tuskegee for weeks," Norrell writes. The threats were credible, too. "A white man living not far from the town had vowed to turn his shotgun on the famous black man, in relaxed confidence that any jury in Alabama would rule the murder a justifiable homicide."

Throughout his tenure, Washington had to steer a prudent course between black advancement and the often vicious opposition of white southerners, including, he realized, a large number of haters in his own vicinity. He sought to produce results not through political officeholding but principally through his educational leadership at Tuskegee.

Washington's animating vision held that individuals who can do what "the world wants done" will prosper, "regardless of race." A young fellow, he said, might venture into a settlement to teach Greek grammar. If, however, the residents perceive no immediate need for the analysis of Greek texts, but they do require houses, bricks, and wagons, then someone able to supply the latter should do well, in fact far better than the learned classicist. Thousands of impoverished African American communities in the rural South benefited from the work of the Tuskegee Institute.

Washington emphasized useful learning, according to which the pure sciences and the applied sciences were never far apart. At Tuskegee, students studied standard grammar, good speaking and writing skills, history, geography, and mathematics. But as Washington explains in his book *Working with the Hands* (1904), students applied the knowledge they'd acquired from the natural sciences and mathematics "to agriculture, cooking, and dairying; not merely geometry and physics, but their application to blacksmithing, brickmaking, farming, and what not." Washington notes that the institute's faculty and leaders "wanted to be careful not to educate our students out of sympathy with agricultural life."

Tuskegee students also learned manners, moral discipline, and good hygiene. Washington believed that the way to improve the nation was to improve oneself. "Character, not circumstances, makes the man," he asserted. As at the University of Virginia, students at Tuskegee learned the virtue—or reinforced the habit—of honesty by telling the truth and respecting others' property. They learned the virtue of temperance by exercising self-discipline and seeing the results. They learned the virtue of industry by working hard and gaining a sense of mastery. The proof of scientific hypotheses is in the testing and in their real-world application. The evidence for moral truth-claims is in the living. In both cases, the propositions' meaning comes out not in the theory but in the doing.

Washington's view was that if someone gained a skill so that he was better at it than anyone else—if he "learned to do a common thing in an uncommon manner"—then, regardless of his color, he would earn the respect of others. Washington opposed unjustly depriving the African American of the right to vote, but he believed that "political agitation alone would not save him." The African American, he said, "must have property, industry, skill, economy, intelligence, and character." A race lacking these attributes would never succeed.

Washington made these points in a major address at the opening of the Cotton States and International Exposition in Atlanta, Georgia, on September 18, 1895. He began by telling the story of a ship lost at sea that finally sighted a friendly vessel and signaled: "Water, water; we die of thirst!" The answer, eventually heeded, was "Cast down your bucket where you are," for the lost vessel had drifted into the mouth of the Amazon River, where the water was fresh.

Washington implored members of his own race to cast down their bucket where they were, in the South. He urged them to make friends among "the people of all races by whom we are surrounded." And take advantage of opportunities close to home in "agriculture, mechanics,...commerce,...domestic service, and...the professions." Most of us, he noticed, must live by the products of our labor. Consequently, "we shall prosper in proportion as we learn to dignify and glorify common labour and put brains and skill into the common occupations of life." African Americans, he pointed out, will do well if they "draw the line between the superficial and the substantial, the ornamental gewgaws of life and the useful." As much dignity resides in "tilling a field as in writing a poem." He believed that "it is at the bottom of life we must begin, and not at the top." That's where students at both Hampton and Tuskegee started, and Washington believed it did them no harm.

He exhorted the white race, also, to "cast down your bucket where you are." Combine the interests of both races, "inter-lacing our industrial, commercial, civil, and religious life with yours." Washington was speaking not of social integration but of linked commercial interests and hiring practices, which could lead to "mutual progress." He asked that any efforts to "curtail the fullest growth of the Negro" be "turned into stimu-lating, encouraging, and making him the most useful and intelligent citizen." African Americans, he averred, could be either one-third "of the ignorance and crime of the South" or "one-third of its intelligence and progress."

The "wisest" members of Washington's race understood, he continued, "that the agitation of questions of social equality is the extremest folly." Although it was only right that "all priv-ileges of the law be ours," it was "vastly more important that we be prepared for the exercise of these privileges." African Americans had a greater need to earn a dollar in a factory than to spend a dollar at the opera. Above even material prosperity, Washington noted, was a "higher good," which was moral and spiritual. He looked forward to the "blotting out of sectional differences and racial animosities," to the administration of "absolute justice," and to the "willing obedience" of "all classes to the mandates of law."

This address drew widespread praise at first. Washington received a telegram from a young professor at Wilberforce University who had only recently become the first African

American to earn a doctorate from Harvard: W. E. B. Du Bois (1868–1963). Du Bois wrote, "Let me heartily congratulate you upon your phenomenal success at Atlanta—it was a word fitly spoken." The young academic also sent a letter to the *New York Age*, a prominent African American newspaper, hailing Washington's speech as the potential "basis of a real settlement between whites and blacks in the South."

But Du Bois and others came to see Washington's ideas as surrendering too much to the existing white power structure. In 1903, Du Bois pejoratively renamed Washington's address the "Atlanta Compromise." The denigration endured. Washington's speech was ridiculed, for instance, in Ralph Ellison's classic novel *Invisible Man* (1952).

By the late 1960s, many African Americans viewed Washington as someone who had sold out his people in exchange for power and influence. They believed that his methods had delayed civil and political rights for blacks. Understandably, they viewed him from the vantage point of Martin Luther King Jr.'s courageous efforts and experiences—boycotts, marches, jailings—and found Washington deficient.

More recently, historians have sought to restore Washington to his complete historical setting. Norrell, in his biography, cautions against the "fallacy of anachronism," which led observers to apply "1960s expectations of protest to a man who had lived two generations earlier." As Norrell points out, "Neither politics nor protest worked in the South of 1895 or 1901 or even 1915." Washington took the most direct route available to him: improvement of African Americans' lives through academic achievement and financial progress.

In his philosophy and strategy, represented in the Atlanta Exposition speech, Washington was sailing in challenging currents. Without renouncing civil or political rights for

African Americans, he recognized the futility—and extreme danger—of agitating for these causes in the South. Tacking close to the shore of apparent accommodation, he sought to come about and gain momentum toward the goal of black economic development, family well-being, and self-esteem. He knew that African Americans could not produce all the wind energy needed to get fully under way. They would immensely benefit if a large portion of this motive power came from their white neighbors. Washington was for equal rights, but he knew that in this era in the deep South, he must pursue justice prudently, sometimes hiddenly, often by indirection. He said, "I could stir up a race war in Alabama in six weeks if I chose," but he knew that doing so "would wipe out the achievements of decades of labor."

And yet Washington worked to undermine discrimination more than contemporaries realized or later generations credited him for. In *Black Rednecks and White Liberals*, the African American economist Thomas Sowell notes that Washington "understood that open challenges to racial discrimination had to be made." Washington wrote to one of the founders of the NAACP, Oswald Garrison Villard, observing that "there is work to be done which no one placed in my position can do." Sowell reminds us that Du Bois was simply not aware of all the moves that Washington was making in secret.

We now have a better picture of Washington's manifold efforts against injustice. He resisted discrimination against blacks by railroads (a source of consistent humiliation), in the jury process, in housing, in voting, in the media, and in other settings. He often wrote and spoke against lynching. Moreover, using his influence and his access to financial resources, he obtained funding for challenges to Jim Crow laws and to invest in African American newspapers. In his June 1913

Atlantic article "The Negro and the Labor Unions," he notes that in some cases, "Negroes are expressly excluded from membership in the unions." He points to occupations in which white workers seek to have black workers fired. He says that white firemen working for railroads try to have black firemen assigned to the worst routes.

Such realities complicate what Sowell calls "the contemporary habit of reducing serious issues and historic figures to the dimensions of cartoon characters." In reality, Sowell says, Washington and Du Bois had "overlapping goals" but "different emphases." Both men—not just Washington—saw an "enormous need for self-improvement among blacks at this juncture in history." Both men—not just Du Bois—believed in higher education in the liberal arts for blacks who would benefit from it. After all, Washington served as a trustee of both Howard and Fisk universities, and he helped channel financial gifts to Talladega College (Alabama), Atlanta University, and other black institutions of higher learning. Washington was for holding no one back, declaring, "I would say to the black boy what I would say to the white boy: get all the mental development that your time and pocket-book will allow of." He affirmed, "We need professional men and women."

Sowell underscores the importance of a historical figure's standpoint. Du Bois, while acknowledging the need of vocational training for many African Americans, focused on academic education for the "talented tenth," men and women who would go on to lead political campaigns for civil rights. Washington saw his "primary task as 'the promotion of progress among the many,'" rather than among the few African Americans in the cultural elite.

Like Sowell, other black intellectuals—including such respected figures as Jason L. Riley, Walter Williams, and

Shelby Steele—have stated reasons to appreciate Washington's role. They are attracted in particular by his positive depiction of African Americans as agents, not victims alone. And they affirm his highlighting of black strengths, resilience, and progress even in the teeth of poverty, hatred, and injustice.

Of course, questions still surround Washington's tactics in the Atlanta Exposition speech, as well as his policy choices in general. And no single exemplar has all the answers. But Washington's virtues and accomplishments—as well as the questions about his approach—remain worthy of attention in our own time. How, then, should a teacher today engage students in a discussion on Booker T. Washington?

As someone teaching the text of his Atlanta speech or *Up from Slavery*, you have the benefit of being an instructor rather than a candidate for political office. You are not expected either to affirm every point Washington made more than a century ago or to condemn his opinions root and branch.

Instead, you might start by taking the following steps:

1. Introduce students to this major figure, his approach, his deeds, and his principles.
2. Paint in the setting: his historical context, especially in the region of Tuskegee, Alabama, in the late nineteenth and early twentieth centuries, when racist New South regimes erected formidable roadblocks to equal justice for all and lynching was carried out with impunity.
3. Fairly represent and discuss other positions, such as those of the northern black intelligentsia, including Du Bois, a civil-rights leader who moved toward black nationalism.
4. Analyze Washington's work in relation to the virtue of prudence.

Josef Pieper's discussion of prudence can inform your discussion. In *The Four Cardinal Virtues*, Pieper stresses, first, the close relationship between prudence and justice. Prudence helps justice find the proper occasion for the correct action on behalf of fair play and the realization of our mutual obligations.

Second, he says, prudence is always oriented to the actual. Therefore it is committed not to what sounds best in theory but to what can be done in fact, and in a timely manner. "Realization of the good," Pieper notes, "presupposes that our actions are appropriate to the real situation." Prudence must be committed to the domain of realistic goals and practical methods. Its scope is the limited world of "down-to-earth realities."

Third, prudence incorporates *providentia*, foresight. It gains as clear a sense as it can of what conditions are and of what is likely to occur on adoption of a specific course of action.

Fourth and finally, no one's prudence is perfect. Concerned as it is with decisions that are by their very nature, in Pieper's words, "concrete, contingent, and future," prudence cannot grant certainty. For this reason, a posture of certitude—the sure conviction that one is absolutely right—should be avoided.

In the light of these features of prudence and of actual conditions in the sharecropper South, students should consider what, if any, application Washington's ideas might have to present-day America, where the political, legal, educational, and social landscape is immensely changed but major problems persist. Which strategies make the most sense, and who should be the primary actors in this work? What does Washington—with his conservative emphasis on education, character, free enterprise, and family stability—have to say to the present?

Booker T. Washington can be an exemplar for students in one other way: as a model of analysis and methodology.

When speaking out against lynching, for example, Washington carefully analyzed the data on this hideous practice. In 1907, Washington published his research on the economic progress of African Americans since the end of slavery. He found that despite the extreme disparities in educational and economic opportunity that blacks faced under both slavery and Jim Crow, the rate of African American homeownership grew from nearly zero in 1860 to 20 percent in 1900. In fact, among all homeowners, a higher percentage of blacks than whites completely owned their own homes.

Washington's approach reminds students to consider policy in the cool light of relevant facts, not in response to emotion, conventional wisdom, or good intentions.

Three Exemplars of Virtue

The differences between our three inspirators are apparent. What they had in common was that all three displayed courage, took on significant challenges, persevered through adversity, and achieved major positive results.

Both Hannah More and George Washington were Anglicans. But, unlike George Washington, both More and Booker T. Washington (a Baptist) were educators who stood within the circle of evangelical Protestantism, although each leaned more toward its practical than its emotional expression. In their ecumenical outlook, all three were irenic, although More had to be concerned about adherence to the Established Church and the rubrics of the prayer book. Each understood and stressed the virtues, especially their application. And all three, in varying degrees, spent time thinking and writing about character.

Another feature they shared is important, as well. After their personalities had jelled—George Washington once past his impetuous youth, Hannah More after she turned toward education and reform, Booker T. Washington following his training at the Hampton Institute—they embodied integrity. They were honest and upright individuals; their characters displayed unity and focus. This integrity—or wholeness—did not make them perfect, and it did not exclude further growth. But it did translate into sincerity and reliability. And this personal strength contributed to their success.

What happens in a person who lacks integrity? How is it lost? How can a person become self-deceived, fractured, and morally adrift, lacking a sense of personal and professional responsibility? To begin this inquiry, we shall look at Robert Penn Warren's tale about a southern populist governor and his retinue: *All the King's Men.*

7

LITERATURE
AND FILM

While history provides a rich source of exemplars, it is by no means the only way to teach the virtues. Excellent novels and films can be prolegomena or adjuncts to nonfiction studies of character. Exploring literature and film with students offers good opportunities to shape the moral imagination.

Consider these examples: two novels and two films.

All the King's Men (1946): Integrity

It's as if Robert Penn Warren wrote this classic American novel principally for high school and college students. With a bit of background supplied by you, the instructor, they will understand the philosophical and psychological theories that a central character, Jack Burden, has in mind when he transforms

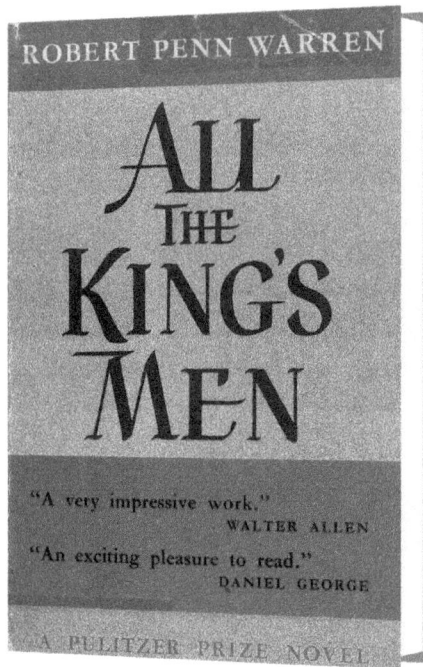

All the King's Men *and the "agony of will"*

them into excuses for his morally questionable behavior—in fact, as rationalistic covers for his flights from personal responsibility. Through this book, students will not only gain a sense of what to avoid; they will also receive insights into what to affirm: personal agency and individual responsibility.

After Jack Burden has gone to work as an assistant to the Boss, Governor Willie Stark, he finds that his new job draws on the skills he acquired as a graduate student—that is, as a PhD candidate "in American history, in the State University of his native state." If your pupils feel a need to pin down this vague reference with more precise historical details implied but never stated, then they might picture Jack as an intelligent young man who had intended to complete his dissertation at Louisiana State University in Baton Rouge, where Robert Penn Warren once taught.

When Chapter 1 begins, in 1936, Jack has been away from his doctoral thesis for more than a decade. In the intervening period, he worked as a newspaperman before becoming an aide to Governor Stark. Jack had an excellent topic for his dissertation, and he had made commendable progress toward completing it. But he faced an obstacle that amounted to more than the usual writer's block: he could not allow the significance of what he had found in his research to touch his inner core. So he keeps trying to run away from what his dissertation implies, even as his research and writing stays with him physically.

The large package containing the hard copy of his thesis travels with Jack in his itinerant existence. The brown paper wrapped around the parcel has turned yellow. The cords that tie the paper together have loosened. The letters *Mr. Jack Burden* printed on the outside have faded, just as the author of this manuscript is fading out as a human being, becoming more and more alienated, unwilling to accept his past and commit himself to the future.

The story's narrator speculates about Jack's situation: "Or perhaps he laid aside [his dissertation] not because he could not understand [the words and the life of the man he was writing about], but because he was afraid to understand, for what might be understood there was a reproach to him." A reproof because Jack lacks integrity: he is not yet a mature, unified individual, honest with himself and with others, an ethically sound human being. This novel is as much about him and his long-delayed effort to get himself together as it is about the protagonist, Willie Stark.

Governor Stark is a left-wing populist. His ends are good: building much-needed hospitals, roads, and schools to assist the poor and the working classes, whom previous administrations had neglected. But his means are foul: bribery, blackmail, coercion. He is a powerful but demagogic speaker. Jack's main task is to hunt for buried political treasure, to employ the research tools he developed at the university and as a reporter to uncover scandals involving the Boss's opponents: state legislators, candidates for office, and their powerful backers.

If there was one useful bit of knowledge that the child Willie Stark picked up in his Presbyterian Sunday school, it was the doctrine of original sin. As governor, Stark assures Jack that diligent investigation will find dirt even on the most upright opponent: "Man is conceived in sin and born in corruption and he passeth from the stink of the didie to the stench of the shroud. There is always something."

Jack does the Boss's bidding—at a cost to his own integrity. To avoid acknowledging the price he's paying, he employs intellectualization, a defense mechanism that removes the annoying burr under his conscience. A prime example occurs in Chapter 1, when the governor and his entourage conduct a photo op at Willie's boyhood home, Old Man Stark's place out in the country. As Jack leans on a fence, he can feel the pint of whiskey he's carrying in his hip pocket. He takes a pull on the bottle and hears someone open and shut the gate to the barn lot.

But Jack doesn't turn around to look at the person. He believes that if he does not see whoever used the gate, he can keep the action out of his mind—and thus the event will not be real. "If I didn't look around it would not be true that somebody had opened the gate with the creaky hinges." He refers to this philosophical insight as "a wonderful principle" and recalls that he had read about it in "a book when I was in college, and I had hung on to it for grim death."

Jack attributes his success in life to this principle: "It had put me where I was." The essence of this position is that "what you don't know don't hurt you, for it ain't real." In his assigned undergraduate textbook, probably for Philosophy 101, the author, Jack says, refers to this mode of thought as Idealism. Finding this metaphysical theory helpful, Jack becomes a "brass-bound Idealist." This philosophical perspective allows Jack to escape moral accountability: "If you are an Idealist it does not matter what you do or what goes on around you because it isn't real anyway."

Jack has learned just enough about philosophical idealism to be irresponsible. Made famous by such exponents as the Anglican bishop and philosopher George Berkeley (1685–1753), this theory holds that no reality exists outside of the mind. There are no material objects, only minds and ideas in minds. James Boswell reports that Samuel Johnson critiqued Berkeley's philosophy by kicking a large stone and declaring, "I refute it *thus!*"

Later in the novel, Jack seizes on another defense to ward off a lacerating sense of his own culpability. He has discovered that the girlfriend of his youth, Anne Stanton, has been having an affair with Governor Stark. Jack cannot face his failures with Anne or recognize the defects of his own character that caused them. He runs away, heading out west, rather than admit to himself that his immaturity as well as his recent opposition research (partly implicating Anne's father, a revered governor of the state) helped to propel Anne into the arms of a strong and charismatic, if flawed, leader.

Some reasons for Jack's personal deficits are not hard to trace. His mother married a string of men who were woefully inadequate as fathers to Jack: the Scholarly Attorney, the Tycoon, the Count, the Young Executive. Each had a nick-name; none had what Jack needed in a father—a pattern of manly responsibility. Hence Jack's relationship to the Boss as a father surrogate. This family background helps to explain, also, Jack's early marriage—before the book's main events— to a gorgeous woman who was better at making the physical adjustments implied by the word *love* than she was at loving or conversing or building any kind of life together.

In the West, Jack spends some time lying on a bed in Long Beach, California. Then he heads home, and he chances upon his new defense mechanism when he stops at a gas station in Don Jon, New Mexico. Encountering an old man with a stiff, leathery face, "as devitalized as the hide on a mummy's jaw," Jack observes a striking feature: "a twitch in the left cheek, up toward the pale-blue eye." What is significant about this spasm is that it is an independent action, "unrelated to the face or to what was behind the face or to anything in the whole tissue of phenomena which is the world we are lost in." This twitch lives "a little life all its own."

From this experience of the man's facial tic, Jack decides he has gained a secret, saving knowledge encompassed in what he calls the Great Twitch theory. Jack has latched on to a descrip-tion of human decision-making and conduct that has taken him beyond true freedom and dignity and into the world of stimulus-response conditioning. This theory is not named, but any student of psychology will recognize it as behaviorism, associated most prominently with the psychologists John B. Watson (1878–1958) and B. F. Skinner (1904–1990). Our behavior, the theory holds, is a response to prior conditioning.

Jack refers to the reactions of the muscle in a frog's leg when the stimulus of an electric current is applied: human responses are just that simple, and just that far removed from the wrestling of conscience and the assertion of free will. Grasping this "mystic vision" of "the Great Twitch" makes Jack feel "clean and free."

Finally, in this novel's concluding sentence, Jack does accept "the awful responsibility of Time," the fact of his personal agency for good or ill. How does he reach this point of moral maturity? The main precipitating factor is an encounter with his own responsibility in a tragic set of circumstances. It's impossible for him to avoid acknowledging his direct involvement in this chain of events.

For our purposes here, however, what's of even greater concern is the reconciliation that occurs between Jack and the subject of his doctoral dissertation, a nineteenth-century southerner called Cass Mastern. Powerfully dramatic, Cass's story takes up all of the fourth of this novel's ten chapters.

Born in north Georgia, Cass joined the Confederate Army, served as a private in the Mississippi Rifles, and came to wear the gray jacket with pride, although he opposed slavery and had vowed never to take the life of another man. His service and his vow were grounded in an effort of expiation, for he believed that he had already taken one life, the life of his friend Duncan Trice, of Lexington, Kentucky, with whose wife, Annabelle, Cass had had an affair several years before the war. Duncan had shot himself through the heart, leaving his wedding band under the pillow on his wife's side of the bed.

This ring was found not by his wife, however, but by—in Annabelle's phrase—the "yellow wench" Phebe, a house servant. Phebe stared at Mrs. Duncan Trice a long time as she extended her arm toward her mistress and slowly opened her fist to reveal the gold ring, "lying," Annabelle noticed, "in a gold hand." The knowledge revealed in Phebe's steady gaze ensured that she would be sold down the river to Paducah, deeper into slave territory and away from her husband, a slave on a nearby plantation—"and she won't look at me anymore like that," Annabelle assured Cass. Guessing what use a buyer would make of Phebe, Cass told her bitterly, "You got a good price, even for a yellow girl as sprightly as Phebe."

Decades later, Jack Burden reads in Cass's journal of "a general disintegration of which I was the center." Cass writes that the discrete events were weighty: the betrayal of a friend, his responsibility for Duncan's death, the sale of an enslaved woman away from her husband and into debauchery, and the awful change and cold rage in the woman he had loved. Together, these terrible facts pointed to an unavoidable conclusion: "all had come from my single act of sin and perfidy, as the boughs from the bole and the leaves from the bough."

What Jack cannot take in until the end of this novel is a way of understanding different from the various theories he has employed in his gestures of self-protection. The Cass Mastern ethical framework derived from his having learned, in the narrator's words, "that the world is all of one piece...like an enormous spider web and if you touch it, however lightly, at any point, the vibration ripples to the remotest perimeter and the drowsy spider feels the tingle and is drowsy no more."

For Jack to accept this point of view, however, means acknowledging his own responsibility, and "how could Jack Burden, being what he was, understand that?" A meeting with the Boss's successor helps; it is like a mirror held up to Jack's face.

The dénouement of *All the King's Men* includes a crucial scene featuring Tiny Duffy, a lowlife politician who has become governor following the assassination of Willie Stark. In their conference, Jack rejects Tiny's offer of a job in his new administration, tells him he knows Tiny was behind the murder of Governor Stark, and dismisses him contemptuously as the Boss's less-than-human toady. Jack describes walking away from this encounter: "I felt like a million. I had sure-God brought off that scene. I had hit him where he lived. I was full of beans. I had fire in my belly. I was a hero. I was St. George and the dragon, I was Edwin Booth bowing beyond the gas-lights, I was Jesus Christ with the horsewhip in the temple."

But then Jack experiences an acid taste in his mouth: "I suddenly asked myself why Duffy had been so sure I would work for him.... And suddenly I knew that I had tried to make Duffy into a scapegoat for me and to set myself off from Duffy." But he sees that he can't do that, after all. "It was as though in the midst of the scene Tiny Duffy had slowly and like a brother winked at me with his oyster eye and I had known he knew the nightmare truth, which was that we were twins"—bound together not by blood but by their common experience as willing minions of the corrupt Willie Stark.

When Jack finally does accept Cass Mastern's spider-web outlook, he embraces an approach to moral reflection and ethical conduct that has been shaped by experience and secured by clear thinking. He sees that "the man of idea" (not a meta-physical but a moral and political idealist) and "the man of fact" (an amoral realist) "were doomed to destroy each other." Each on his own is a danger to both self and society. A pru-dent method in the political sphere or within any other ethical arena balances principles and conditions.

Jack comes to accept that human beings live "in the agony of will"; they cannot renounce their moral agency but must choose and act as best they can. At the close of the story, during a discussion of "the theory of the moral neutrality of history," Hugh Miller, an honest politician, wisely tells Jack,

"History is blind, but man is not." At last more integrated, mature, and ethically aware, Jack marries Anne Stanton and settles down to write a book about Cass Mastern, "whom once I could not understand but whom, perhaps, I now may come to understand."

Ride the High Country (1962): Loyalty

Starring Joel McCrea and Randolph Scott in their last major screen appearances, this Metro-Goldwyn-Mayer picture introduces a young and manifestly talented Mariette Hartley (playing Elsa Knudsen), and it features an outstanding supporting cast that includes Edgar Buchanan, James Drury, Warren Oates, and L. Q. Jones. Marking the end of the era of the classic Western, it is an elegiac remembrance of virtues past but also a film not without hope for things to come.

Shot in CinemaScope by the first-class cameraman Lucien Ballard in settings that included the Sierra Nevada Mountains, this film has a beauty that is both natural and moral. Following its release in Europe, *Ride the High Country* defeated Federico Fellini's *8½* for first prize at the Belgium Film Festival and won the Paris film critics award for best motion picture. For some critics and viewers, including me, *Ride the High Country*—the film that launched Sam Peckinpah's reputation as an important filmmaker—is even better than Peckinpah's intensely violent, revisionist Western *The Wild Bunch* (1969).

Because the best movies have a multisensory power to bring so much together on the big screen—character development within a carefully paced narrative arc punctuated by sound and silence and illustrated by exactly rendered light and images—films have the capacity to engage our imaginations as no other

Ride the High Country: *code of honor*

medium can. Especially in respect of the moral life, we know that not only the mind but also the volitional and emotional aspects of the self must be involved.

Good films can incite interest, provoke questions, and create memories, which viewers might then employ as touchstones for future cognition. For students of the virtues, *Ride the High Country* crystallizes beliefs and codes of behavior worth analyzing and affirming today. And this film does so not as a didactic artifact but as an absorbing story that reaches out to mind, heart, and will.

Among this movie's widely appreciated episodes, the ending is the most famous: one of the most powerfully evocative death scenes in all of cinema history. It's a scene that marks the death not only of the film's good guy, a former U.S. marshal named Steve Judd (played by McCrea), but also, potentially, of all he has stood for through many years of dedicated service to law and order in the West.

This somber assessment is supported by the film's opening scenes, in which Steve rides into town and mistakenly infers that the cheering throngs are saluting his past glory as a peace officer. Instead, they are whooping it up for a dishonest race between a camel and a horse. It's the early twentieth century, a horseless carriage chugs slowly through the center of town, and a uniformed constable (not a sheriff with a six-gun) yells at Steve, who, after some years of barely scraping by, looks a little the worse for wear in his shabby apparel: "Get out of the way, old man; can't you hear? Can't you see you're in the way?"

In real life, *Ride the High Country* marked all kinds of disappointing closures. But in this film, when Steve dies, the viewer is deeply satisfied that this lawman's principal concern is realized. Earlier in the movie, riding a trail in the mountains with Gil Westrum (Scott), his sidekick from years before, Steve speaks lines that are unabashedly moral—in fact, unselfconsciously religious. To today's audiences, familiar with either overly sentimental or casually dismissive renderings of Christian themes in films (and, interestingly, *Ride the High Country* includes a violent, misshapen Christian, Elsa's father, Joshua Knudsen), the straightforward treatment in this Western might prove a relief.

Gil has decided that society owes him some recompense for his years of serving the cause of frontier justice. Reduced to performing in a carnival as a cheap imitation of a western hero (playing a sharpshooter called the Oregon Kid), Gil has no desire to die a poor man. He plans to steal the gold shipment that he, Steve, and a young man named Heck Longtree (Ron Starr) have been hired to protect on its journey from a mining camp in the High Sierras to the town bank in Hornitos, California.

Gil wants to entice Steve to join him in this theft—it's only stealing from the bank, after all, and they're entitled to the gold after all those years of loyal service, taking bullets for next to nothing. Approaching his theme indirectly, Gil asks Steve: "You know what's on the back of a poor man when he dies? The clothes of pride. And they are not a bit warmer to him dead than they were when he was alive. Is that all you want, Steve?"

But Gil cannot convince his old partner to break his code of honor. Indeed, Steve's ethics appear to have a transcendent status, a metaphysical heft, that more than compensates for the outward shame of his frayed cuffs and threadbare coat. Steve recalls a tough sheriff who set him straight years earlier: "See, he was right, and I was wrong," Steve informs Gil, and "that makes the difference."

"Who says so?" Gil asks.

Steve replies: "Nobody. That's something you just know."

Morality has an objective grounding apart from individual preferences.

On the trail, Steve makes it clear that he's still dedicated to living by this sense of right and wrong, come what may. His reply to Gil's "Is that all you want, Steve?" is "All I want is to enter my house justified." It's a line that Sam Peckinpah, who rewrote much of the original film script, borrowed directly from his father and indirectly from Luke 18:14, in which the humble tax collector (who confesses himself a "sinner"), rather than the Pharisee, went down to his house justified before God.

Toward the end of *Ride the High Country*, a climactic shoot-out takes place in which Steve and Gil team up one last time. They kill the film's villains, but Steve is mortally wounded. Before he dies, his courageous example and the bond between the two men are enough to prompt Gil's turning back to the right path. Gil tells Steve: "Don't worry about anything [that is, what will happen not only to the gold but also, by extension, to Gil]. I'll take care of it, just like you would've."

Steve replies: "Hell, I know that. I always did. You just forgot it for a while, that's all." When Steve tells Gil, "So long," he pauses for a moment and then adds "partner."

Steve's gracious word of acceptance springs from his Christian character, which apparently took shape following his own experience years earlier of being set right and given a fresh start. Without hesitating, Steve responds to Gil by expressing his abiding confidence in his friend's underlying worth; his trust and loyalty summon and affirm the best in Gil.

Reconciled at the end to Steve, Gil tells his old partner, in the film's final line: "I'll see you later." Spoken in this scene, these words, which otherwise might be heard as a trite phase of farewell or of casual consolation, instead convey a real hope. Then, in his last moments, alone, Steve turns his head to face the mountains, and there can be little question that, although a sinner, he will enter his house justified.

There's nothing flashy or moralistic about Steve Judd. He accepts ethical uncertainty—right and wrong are not always easy to discern—but he takes a moral view of the created order and of his role in it. He embraces the virtues of leadership: moral and physical courage, humility, self-mastery, and trustworthiness, even in the face of changing times and in a world of conflicting values. He believes in honesty at all costs, in service and self-sacrifice.

Whether these sorts of individuals are only for the past is a decision that each student must make for himself or herself. What Sam Peckinpah's 1962 motion picture offers all of us is an unforgettable invitation to ride the high country.

Darkness at Noon (1941): Faith

In Chapter 5, we encountered faith as trust and loyalty. We saw that in absolute faith, the focus of devotion is not simply a person's highest good but also that which determines the significance and merit of everything else. If x is a person's object of faith, then he will depend on x—in the words of H. Richard Niebuhr—"not only for his own meaning but for the worth of everything else he encounters." And he will be loyal to x no matter what resistance he encounters and at whatever cost to himself. Each finite entity—truth, life, honor, personal relationships—takes on its meaning and worth only relative to this ultimate center of value.

Which is precisely what we find in *Darkness at Noon*, the novel by Arthur Koestler (an active member of the Communist Party from 1932 to 1938) about the Soviet show trials of 1936–1938. Part of a larger campaign of terror, this ruthless purge of the party's upper ranks was General Secretary Joseph Stalin's way of eliminating potential rivals and securing his power. Neither Stalin nor the Union of Soviet Socialist Republics nor the Communist Party is mentioned in Koestler's book; they are referred to instead as No. 1 and the Country of the Revolution and the Party.

The main figure in *Darkness at Noon*—the title alludes to Job 5:14—is the Old Bolshevik Nikolai Salmanovich Rubashov, a hero of the Russian Civil War and a former

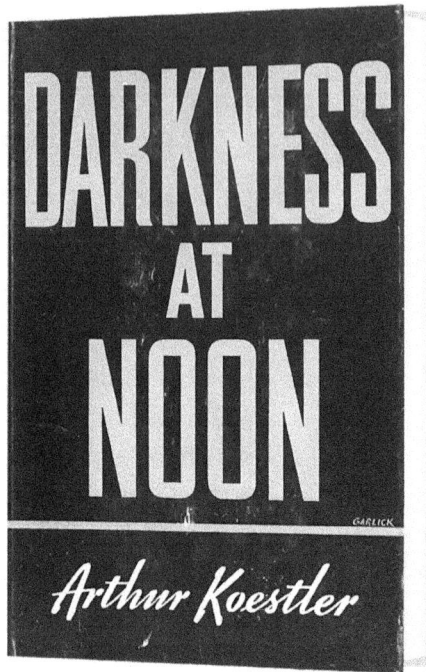

Darkness at Noon: *the object of faith as the ultimate center of value*

high-ranking Communist Party official. He is arrested on the orders of No. 1, imprisoned, interrogated, and finally executed for committing counterrevolutionary crimes.

Although he is not guilty of the specific charges laid against him, in his prison cell he remembers those he treated shabbily in the name of rigid party discipline. His victims include his secretary and former lover, Arlova. Because Rubashov testified against her even though she was innocent, he feels responsible for her subsequent execution.

Recalling these former comrades and his ruthless participation in the events that led to their deaths, he is bothered more and more by a nascent conscience, represented by his damaged eye-tooth, which causes a pain in his upper-right jaw. Significantly, it is the *eye*-tooth that is causing his trouble. When he visits the prison infirmary, his tooth does not ache. But then the doctor starts probing with his finger (*ah!*), and Rubashov turns pale and has to lean against a wall. "There it is!" the doctor exclaims. "The root of the right eye-tooth is broken off and has remained in the jaw."

Although Rubashov at one point had at least the beginnings of a sound conscience, he was converted to Marxist-Leninist dogma, and traditional morality broke off. But its root remains. This long-submerged, now awakening, ethical sense is not enough, however, to stand up to his interrogators' demands. Even though, having witnessed Communism's real-world effects, he has grown skeptical of the party's theories and methods, he signs the confession his masters want. He subscribes his name to this document because party values— reflecting the principles and aims of the ongoing revolution— retain a dominant hold on his thinking. He is aware of harboring oppositional thoughts, and he still wants to serve the Communist cause.

Thus, for Rubashov, "bourgeois" ethics, the norms of "cricket morality," weak and undeveloped, yield to the revolutionary moral code. The latter, he realizes, comprises the ethics of a millennial movement that is wholly "without scruples." The only crime—or sin—it recognizes is that of deviation: swerving from the course that History has laid out. The sole punishment is death, about which there is "nothing exalted." Death is simply "the logical solution to political divergences."

According to the religion of the Communist Party, "the old man with the slanting Tartar eyes" (V. I. Lenin) is revered as God the Father, and No. 1 (Stalin) is honored as the Son. But the real center of value is not any one human being but rather the dialectical process in history, discerned by the chosen few in the party leadership. This god is not a personal deity but an impersonal cosmic force, indifferent to individual persons.

In relation to this center of value, nothing has independent worth or meaning. During his interrogation, Rubashov and his inquisitors don't distinguish between actual deeds he carried out and notional acts he entertained in consequence of his deviationist views. Thus the usual distinctions between reality and appearance and between fact and fiction break down. His interrogator Gletkin clarifies what the party means by "truth": it "is what is useful to humanity, falsehood what is harmful." Rubashov explains what this perspective on truth amounts to in practice: "We whip the groaning masses of the country toward a theoretical future happiness which only we can see." Ultimately, No. 1, subservient only to the dictates of History as he perceives them, determines what is true according to this utilitarian calculus.

The Communists see the ethics of "fair play" or basic justice—giving to each person his or her due as a human being—as outdated: "the nineteenth century's liberal ethics." Revolutionary ethics represent modern, twentieth-century norms. For example, because No. 1 is taken to be infallible, when he decreed that potash is superior to nitrate artificial manure, and B., the leading agricultural research scientist, said the opposite, B. had to be shot, along with thirty of his colleagues who agreed with him. It didn't matter that B. was arguing in good faith and could well have been right about the facts. "History has taught us that often lies serve her better than the truth." The great masses of the people are sluggish and need to be lied to in order to entice them to accept the larger truths of revolutionary socialism. Justice and truth take on meaning only relative to the center of value, which is the unfolding of history toward an imminent paradisiacal future.

Interestingly enough, this outlook also necessitates a reevaluation of honor. Confined in the cell next to Rubashov's, No. 402 is a czarist and a former army officer. When Rubashov tells him he is capitulating, 402 says he'd rather hang, and asks him: "Have you no spark of honour left?"

Rubashov replies that "our ideas of honour differ."

No. 402 quickly taps out a definition of honor: "Honour is to live and die for one's belief."

To which Rubashov responds: "Honour is to be useful without vanity."

No. 402's basic moral stance is the old-fashioned view that ethics are deontological: individuals' actions should conform to established precepts, laws, and prohibitions, no matter what the motivation to act otherwise. Persons are bound (*deon*) to obey these standards of right and wrong. For example, students—and military officers—ought to comply with the rules of their body's honor code: always tell the truth, do not steal, never cheat.

Rubashov's ethics, on the other hand, are radically utilitarian: we should put aside the outdated scruples that people like 402 cling to out of personal "vanity" and instead strive always to be objectively "useful," by working strenuously to effect whatever the party says will realize the greatest good for the greatest number. And we should pursue this course remorselessly, taking on board the lies that must be told and the murders that must be committed along the way. As Ivanov declares to Rubashov: "The principle that the end justifies the means is and remains the only rule of political ethics." But Rubashov is aware of the results when this single norm is applied. Communist ethics, he knows, are "so consequent, that in the interest of a just distribution of land we deliberately let die of starvation about five million farmers and their families in one year."

The problem with this ethical stance is signaled, as well, in the epigraph to this novel's last chapter, titled "The Grammatical Fiction," in these lines by the German philosopher, jurist, and politician Ferdinand Lassalle (1825–1864):

Show us not the aim without the way,
For ends and means on earth are so entangled
That changing one, you change the other too;
Each different path brings other ends in view.

In other words, show us not the end without presenting the means, too, for if your methods are execrable, then you will be less likely to attain your valued goal or achieve a just result.

No. 402's definition of honor also reflects his commitment to the worth of each person: "live and die *for one's belief.*" The Communist's utilitarian ethics reject this attention to the first-person singular in favor of the hypothetical good of the masses. But Rubashov's throbbing eye-tooth suggests not only the inner eye of conscience but also, relatedly, the "I" of personal identity and self-awareness. At one point he asks his interrogator Ivanov, "Why actually do you people intend to have me shot?"

Ivanov bristles at Rubashov's locution: "Listen, Rubashov. There is one thing I would like to point out to you. You have now repeatedly said 'you'—meaning State and Party, as opposed to 'I'—that is...Rubashov." The correct way of thinking and therefore the standard form of expression is to say "we," referring to the collective, represented by the party. As Rubashov observes in one of his discussions with Ivanov, in the Communist system, "respect for the individual and social progress are incompatible."

Rubashov's exchange with No. 402 about honor points to another lacuna in the former's morality: the absence in his life of what Edmund Burke calls "just prejudice." Hence, Rubashov "envied" men like 402 because their "rigid code of honour prescrib[ed] how to live and how to die. To that one could cling." For Rubashov and all true believers in the socialist utopia, the situation is otherwise: "there was no text-book; everything had to be worked out."

And therein lies half the problem. Morality is completely relative, consequentialist, and ungrounded. Justice is conjured up on the spot and inevitably constructed to suit the inter-ests of the stronger. No. 402, a prisoner of the state who is one of the few remaining "authentic counter-revolutionaries," personifies honor as traditional virtue: acting according to time-honored ethical principles, in line with what C. S. Lewis calls the Tao. No. 402 thereby incurs the hostility of the party apparatchiks, servants of the coldest and most pernicious variety of teleological ethics. From the perspective of a mod-ern revolutionary, No. 402's "narrow conception of honour belonged to another epoch."

Toward the end, Rubashov appears to question the sterile logic of the Revolution: "the running-amuck of pure reason." He concludes: "Perhaps it did not suit man to be completely freed from old bonds, from the steadying brakes of 'Thou shalt not' and 'Thou mayst not,' and to be allowed to tear along straight towards the goal." But his insights arrive too late. His and his associates' faith in the god that failed has produced catastrophic results for tens of millions of human beings.

Homo sapiens is also ineluctably *homo religiosus*, which is not an unadulteratedly good thing. As Roger Scruton told the philosopher Mark Dooley: "Once the idols have been brought to earth, individual freedom, and the flesh which harbours it, become *property*. They can be placed in the balance of calculation, and discarded 'for the public good.'" Mindful of the ambiguity of faith, we may be better positioned to guard against placing absolute trust in and awarding total loyalty to idols. Faith trusts—and faith doubts.

The Hanging Tree (1959): Hope

When we first see him, he is riding a horse through stunning country: the Oak Creek Wildlife Area, northwest of Yakima, Washington, standing in for the Montana of the 1860s–1870s Gold Rush. It is 1873, and the horseman, played by Gary Cooper starring in his last Western, is leading a packhorse, laden with supplies and a shingle bearing his name, "Joseph Frail, M.D." As he rides slowly along the mountain trail toward his destination, Skull Creek, he looks up at a gnarled oak tree. Suspended from it is a rope with a freshly cut, frayed end. A local resident proclaims with boosterish enthusiasm, "Every new mining camp's got to have its hanging tree; makes folks feel respectable!"

Doc Frail buys a prospector's cabin and soon rescues and treats a young sluice robber, named Rune (Ben Piazza), wounded in his attempt to get away from the miners who pursued him. With Rune as with others in this raw village, Frail has to be in control. Having extracted a bullet of an unusual caliber from Rune's chest, he makes the young man his bondservant until he can pay off his fee. Frail requires him to work, under threat of exposure, "for as long as I say, maybe forever."

The Hanging Tree: *hope and the assistance of others*

When Doc starts treating patients, he attracts the antagonism of another "doctor," George Grubb (George C. Scott, in his film debut), a faith healer who advertises, "Your fortune told by the Bible, 50¢" and "Expert laying on of hands." Concerned about losing business, Grubb declaims about Frail: "The butcher doctor! His instruments are foul with sin!"

In fact, Frail is not only a medical man but also a gambler and a gunslinger, with a mysterious past. One evening at the saloon, he is playing cards and wins a large pot, including a mining claim, from Society Red (John Dierkes), who asks him: "What are you going to do with all that, Doc? Buy a ticket to Illinois and burn down another house?" Frail punches Red in the face and draws his revolver on him. Rune, who observes the scene, later tells him, "If you ain't the devil, he's sure sittin' on your shoulder."

But in this fine example of a 1950s-style, "psychological" Western, matters are more involved than they appear. On a search for a "lost lady" thrown from a stagecoach after a robbery, one of the decent fellows in town, Tom Flaunce (Karl Swenson), who has known Frail for about five years, tells Rune more about him. The doc, he says, could have had it "rich and easy" where he used to live, but he keeps moving on with his doctor's bag. "Once I asked [him] about that name of his. All he said was it suited a man with frail hope." His real name is Temple, and he lived in a "fine grand house on a point that overlooked the joining of the rivers," where the Ohio runs into the Mississippi. But "something happened in the house one night. They say that a man and a woman were killed. And the doctor put the torch to the house and burned it to the ground. You can still see the burned chimney sticking up above the willows where the rivers meet."

Soon, Frenchy Plante (Karl Malden), one of the most despicable characters in this frontier oasis, finds the lost lady, Elizabeth Mahler (Maria Schell), and yells: "Me, me, I found her—me!" She suffers from second-degree burns, dehydration, a possible concussion, and temporary blindness. They take her to recover in a house owned—but no longer lived in—by Tom and Edna Flaunce, just across from the doctor's cabin. One of the community's busybodies, Edna (Virginia Gregg) declares: "She's hardly in the hands of a saint, you know. If she's decent, she doesn't belong up there." When she and several other ladies try to visit the patient, the doc doesn't let them inside. Elizabeth asks Frail's indentured servant, "Am I a prisoner, Rune?" And he answers, "The doc tells everybody what to do."

Frenchy manages to gain access to Elizabeth's temporary home when she is alone. He grabs her, but she fends him off.

When the doctor discovers what has happened, he goes to confront Frenchy at the saloon. In front of many witnesses, the latter notifies Frail that he's carrying no weapon. They fight outside in the street. After defeating Frenchy, the doctor promises him, "If I ever find you on that hill again, it makes no difference if you're wearing a gun or not, I'll kill you." Grubb declares, "I warn you again: that butcher is the devil, and you must cast him out!" And Red observes, salaciously, "Looks like the doc's going to keep the little lady all to himself." Frenchy affirms that "one of these days" he'll take his revenge. Confronting Frail, Rune says: "You don't own her! Is that how it was before? You tried to own somebody until they hated you?"

The truth about "how it was before" comes out after Elizabeth is restored to health and falls in love with Frail. But he spurns her advances and tells her she's leaving Skull Creek the next morning on the eastbound stage. When she asks him where she can go, he replies: "Wherever people go when they know they've come the wrong way. There's no place for you here." She doesn't understand, and says: "You will not again tell me what to do and what not to do."

She, Frenchy, and Rune go in as partners in prospecting for gold. But Frenchy won't keep his hands off her: "Don't a partner have some rights, heh? Don't even get a free look?" Then Elizabeth learns that Doc is subsidizing their effort. Edna Flaunce, who informs her of this fact, goes on to tell her: "Ain't none of us have to ask how you've been paying him back, kept...like any harlot."

Elizabeth tells Frail about this conversation and says he is cruel in the way he draws people to him and then turns them away if they get too close. "Do you love to torture?"

He replies, "No, I don't."

She asks if it's true that his wife killed herself. He acknowledges that it is and that the man who died with her was his brother. The implication is that the two had been lovers.

Elizabeth and her partners strike gold, and Frenchy lets his newfound riches go to his head. He throws a party, free drinks for all, while the doc is out of town tending to the injured at a mine disaster. The psychopath Grubb starts fires around town and is eager to set Doc's place alight. Amid these riotous goings-on, Frenchy takes advantage of Doc's departure to seek out Elizabeth, telling her, "Frenchy's waited long enough."

When she screams, he hits her and attempts to force himself on her. Just then, Doc returns home, hears her struggling under her crazed partner's assault, bounds up the steps two at a time, throws Frenchy down the staircase, and turns to aid Elizabeth. Downstairs, Frenchy grabs a gun out of a holster and fires up at Doc, hitting the wooden railing to his left. Wheeling around at the top of the stairs, Frail draws fast and does not miss. He fires his revolver as Frenchy stumbles out the door. Doc keeps firing outside until Frenchy falls dead at the edge of the cliff. Doc uses his boot to topple Frenchy over the edge onto a rock about twenty yards below.

Seizing his opportunity, Grubb screams: "Murderer! Butcher! Nail him to the tree!" Others yell: "Lynch him! Lynch him!" They take Doc to the hanging tree, and, smiling happily, Grubb secures the rope around his neck. He quotes the Bible: "Whoso sheddeth man's blood, by man shall his blood be shed" (Genesis 9:6a).

Just then, in the distance, we see Rune and Elizabeth hurrying toward the scene. Doc yells at them to "go back!" but they continue on. Elizabeth gains the attention of the mob and tells them: "You can have our gold! You can have everything! Please take it! You even can have our claim!" The gleeful folks grab for the pieces of gold being tossed and scramble for the piece of paper—the valuable mining claim—that's floating on the breeze. It's a scene of unvarnished selfishness and greed. Their base natures on full display, they are totally distracted from the lynching and decide to let Elizabeth have her man if she wants him that badly.

Yet after Rune releases Doc from the noose, Elizabeth turns away from the hanging tree to walk home. Perhaps she figures that she has cleared her debt to him, and he doesn't want her anyway. But then he calls her name, and she goes to him.

Several critics have found this motion picture to be dark and cynical. And certainly most of the leading characters are awful: embodiments of concupiscence, envy, and ignorance. Doc tells Elizabeth that Skull Creek is not fit for her; it contains "some of the scum of the world."

The protagonist's situation is distinct, however. Doc has chosen his new name to signify his lack of hope, and with it the absence of both love and trust. When he arrives on horseback, he is a damaged man, wounded and embittered, without resources other than a jury-rigged carapace for his emotions, ready funds to gamble with, and formidable skills with a scalpel and a six-gun. Traumatized, he will not let anyone come too close. Striving to maintain self-control, he seeks distance from and even mastery over others. Kind and generous toward his patients, he is fine as long as he does not have to be vulnerable. Bearing the wounds of family tragedy, he has no hope of ever making a full recovery.

Which is why Tom Flaunce says that Frail must keep traveling on. But Doc senses that he is moving toward his fate, not his destiny. That perception is revealed more clearly in the work on which the film is based: the novella by

Dorothy M. Johnson (1905–1984), who also wrote the short stories "A Man Called Horse" and "The Man Who Shot Liberty Valance." In Johnson's story, when Frail is riding toward the mining camp and sees the rope on the hanging tree, "his muscles went tense, for he remembered that there was a curse on him."

One characteristic of hope is the anticipation of receiving assistance from someone else. But Doc expects no help from anyone. In a sense, this despair is his curse. Another element of hope entails looking forward to improvement: becoming a different person from who I am right now, better off than I am in this dismal state. Inner or outer conditions—or both—will turn brighter. For the doctor, such prospects are no more than a frail hope. At least he can pursue his vocation as he makes some money on the side. But he can do nothing to save himself, and he looks for little from others.

Then the final scene occurs, and Doc comes close to being hanged: his fate reaching out for him. But Elizabeth rescues him, and, like Jack Burden, Frail cannot resist the force of these new realities. Some of the last words we hear in this film are from its first-rate title song (written by Mack David and Jerry Livingston), sung by Marty Robbins: there's "new hope for me."

Joseph Frail's life is complicated, but the lesson of his story is simple: our moral imaginations require the presence and aid of others if we are to enjoy that confident expectation we call hope. No one has made this crucial point more effectively than William Lynch in his book *Images of Hope*. He rightly notes that we are so used to thinking of our imaginations as wholly private faculties that we run into problems when we need hope. Hope—envisioning fresh possibilities—depends on the resources of our imaginations. What we experience when we lose hope is that "the private imagination, of which we are so enamored, reaches" the end of its reserves. My imagination's well runs dry—I can see only that this burden will be mine forever—and so I experience despair.

My error is to think of my storehouse of images as an isolated unit. The virtue of hope requires a more gregarious imagination than that: hope, as Lynch says, "not only imagines; it *imagines with*." To come upon the answers I need, I "must put on the imagination of another." Otherwise I cannot discover the thread that will lead me out of this maze. Without assistance from others, my imagination, Lynch writes, "is lost." As Doc Frail learns, the virtue of hope cannot be realized alone. His isolated imagination arrives at the end of its rope—all too literally—and can be set free only through the hope of an imaginative other.

Your Turn

I recognize that you may not be interested in teaching any of the four examples I have discussed in this chapter. That is perfectly fine. My purpose here has not been to find the best items for your syllabus. In fact, two American Westerns released within a few years of each other and two World War II–era novels scarcely reflect the rich diversity of literature and cinema. So being careful about selecting representative examples was clearly not my aim, either.

What this chapter does is present a small number of novels and films that I find compelling. I have regularly taught two of these works and would no doubt enjoy teaching all four. So in this chapter I have sought merely to convey the spirit and a bit of the form of this enterprise.

Please, then, rewrite this chapter with your own favorite pieces. And do not let your students speak only of the events (the facts) in each film or novel and of whether they liked the work or identified with its characters. Dive beneath the surface and examine the important character traits involved and their impact in the story. This exercise, if well planned and carried out, will be not only morally constructive but also thoroughly enjoyable.

8

PIETY

E ven more unfashionable than humility and temperance is
the virtue of piety. And yet if, in a Christian school, the
virtues need to venture beyond the sacred precincts of morning prayers to enter into the hustle and bustle of the academic
microcosm in all its variety, at the end of the day they must
return to the chapel, to its altar and Bible, to its pulpit and
pews, in order to receive their orientation and to renew their
distinct purpose.

The meaning of the virtues for members of the school
community begins and ends in the chapel, for without being
embedded in the complete narrative of creation, fall, redemp-
tion, and sanctification, the virtues falter in a fragmented
cultural environment, or they end up hanging out with the
wrong gang. They can turn into clumsy or misleading guides.
Piety assists in preventing our being misled. It is a fortification

against the seven deadly sins, which the demonic realm aids and abets: pride, greed, wrath, envy, lust, gluttony, and sloth.

When, inevitably, sins breach this fortification, piety provides occasions for a fresh start. Within the freedom of a church school lies a cornucopia of opportunities to learn to exercise rights and to embrace duties. But all persons, young and old and in between, fall short again and again: "For all have sinned..." (Romans 3:23). Therefore the liturgy offers times for contrition and repentance, mercy and healing, thanksgiving and new strength.

As devotion owed by the radical monotheist, piety represents justice toward the true God and realism about both ourselves and all the false gods of this world. And yet piety does not simply subtend justice, for the debts that we have incurred to our Maker and to our parents cannot be repaid. Piety is a manifestation of our trust in God and an expression of our gratitude for the gifts, including life itself, that we have received. Also, it directs our loyalty to God's cause, inciting our reverence toward the whole created order and our respect for other creatures. In Luke 10, a lawyer asks Jesus, "Who is my neighbor?" And Jesus answers with a story about a "certain man [who] went down from Jerusalem to Jericho" (v. 30). This famous parable of the Good Samaritan points to the triadic relationship of self-God-neighbor.

Recalling a useful term from Simone Weil, we can affirm that the chapel is the place where students, faculty, and leaders can learn and relearn how to give attention where attention is due. As Weil points out, prayer is "attention in its pure form." Teaching the virtues in such a way that they stick—for life—is no easy task, as instructors from Plato to the present have realized. The repetition that formal prayer requires and the focused attention that it supports can help the virtues sink in.

And first in the traditional order of prayer—even before thanksgiving, confession, and supplication—comes adoration, for praise is the necessary starting point of all piety. No prayer that I am aware of more magnificently or memorably draws the attention of the worshiper forward to the throne of grace (Hebrews 4:16) than the *Te Deum laudamus*, which begins:

> We praise thee, O God; we acknowledge thee to be the Lord.
> All the earth doth worship thee, the Father everlasting.
> To thee all Angels cry aloud; the Heavens, and all the Powers therein;
> To thee Cherubim and Seraphim continually do cry,
> Holy, Holy, Holy, Lord God of Sabaoth;
> Heaven and earth are full of the Majesty of thy glory.
> The glorious company of the Apostles praise thee.
> The goodly fellowship of the Prophets praise thee.
> The noble army of Martyrs praise thee.
> The holy Church throughout all the world doth acknowledge thee;
> The Father, of an infinite Majesty.

As a primary expression of piety, the *Te Deum* orients the worshiper, boldly establishing a framework of meaning for the Christian virtues.

Context

The setting of the virtues influences their identification (which ones are included and which are omitted), their prominence (which traits are brought to the fore), and their interpretation (their meaning in context). This fact is well known, and we hardly need to belabor it here. In *After Virtue*, the philosopher Alasdair MacIntyre has much to say about social worlds and varying lists of virtues, such as those of Homer, Aristotle, New Testament Christians, and Benjamin Franklin.

As we have seen, even Rubashov has virtues, settled dispositions deemed appropriate for realizing the goal of the chiliastic cause that he's pledged to: an end state of perfect justice and harmony. He notes that among all the revolutionary virtues there is only one that he never managed to incorporate in his life: "the virtue of self-deception." This faculty—enabling a person to be blind to the consequences of his own foul deeds—would have been psychologically useful when Rubashov was carrying out the Communist Party's instructions in the countries where he operated, Germany and Belgium.

In acknowledging his failure to learn this virtue, he's being ironic, of course, but not about the virtues in general. Communist believers lived lives of faith and hope, of loyalty and self-sacrifice. For party members, the virtue of piety was an orienting trait. In relation to their center of value, they translated and enacted the meanings of faith, truth, justice, hope, life, death, dignity, and honor.

In other spheres, as well, piety performs an orienting function in relation to the other virtues. In their primer on the virtues, Craig Boyd and Kevin Timpe include an excellent chapter on Islamic and Confucian virtues. For Muslims, "the key question is 'What does God require of me?'" And the starting point for all the virtues is "obedience to the commands of Allah." Generosity, justice, and wisdom emerged as essential virtues, and Muslims came to emphasize these good habits directly in relation to God. Generosity, for example, is a response to God the Merciful. We reflect God's gracious nature in our charity and mercy. "By developing virtues we draw close to Allah, bringing about our 'spiritual happiness.'" The virtues, then, are central to the practice of Islam. Submission to Allah entails developing our characters in relation to God's being and goodness.

In Confucianism, too, the virtues are closely related to ultimate spiritual reality: *dao*, or the Way. The character traits stressed are justice, truthfulness, courage, and so forth—but all within a life lived in accord with the *dao*. "Recapturing the *dao*," write Boyd and Timpe, "requires bringing people back to the correct path by cultivating *de*, a dispositional character that is often translated as 'virtue.' *De*... is the manifestation of the *dao* in a virtuous life."

Earlier we said that a suitable working definition of *virtues* was good habits conducing to good ends. Now I would add the orientation provided by piety and the context offered by Christian tradition and community. Virtue's ultimate end is the *telos* of willing the will of God: the alignment of our selfish and often misguided wills with the sovereign, holy will of God, conclusively revealed in the person and work of Jesus Christ.

At the same time, let's keep in mind the theme of this entire book, which is that the virtues, although they start and end each day in the chapel, must leave that sacred space and enter daily existence. Just as in the ancient world the good Roman citizen practiced *pietas*, incorporating in his life not only reverence toward the gods but also proper respect toward parents, kinsmen, and country, so in the modern world, and particularly in our schools, ought we to embody dutifulness toward the natural order, practicing piety personally, civically, and even academically. A kind of reverence is owed to learning itself, to great texts and authors, to knowledge and wisdom accumulated over millennia, to the beauty of creative works

George C. Marshall: soldier and statesman of character

and new discoveries, to the labors of students and teachers, and to academic integrity.

A Final Exemplar: George C. Marshall (1880–1959)

Perceptive about the sources of piety within the bonds that unite us, Edmund Burke would have appreciated Josef Pieper's statement, in *The Four Cardinal Virtues*, that "the world is not to be kept in order through justice alone." Within a web of meaning and mutuality, citizens feel gratitude for what they have received from forebears, and their thankful inclinations motive their concern for future generations. They willingly answer the call of community or country, and duty becomes a habit they do not have to question each time they are challenged to do the right thing. Burke leads us to quiet virtues—prudence, humility, duty, gratitude—that we need to be reminded of in our own time.

We gain a sense of what Burke meant and of his ongoing pertinence when we test his themes in the context of the life of an American general honored for his character as much as for his leadership: George C. Marshall, who personified the virtues of faith, hope, prudence, temperance, courage, humility, patience, and justice. Winston Churchill designated him the "organizer of victory" in World War II. And on June 5, 1947, when Marshall as secretary of state spoke at Harvard University and announced the European Recovery Program (which soon became known as the Marshall Plan), his honorary-degree citation referred to him as "a soldier and statesman whose ability and character brook only one comparison in the history of the nation"—that is, to George Washington.

One of the mediating institutions that most affected Marshall was his home parish, St. Peter's Episcopal Church in Uniontown, Pennsylvania, where he was baptized at six months of age. The Reverend John R. Wightman, the young rector of St. Peter's, made a lasting impression on the future general. Marshall recalled him in a letter that he wrote during the Second World War, on August 6, 1943: "Mr. Wightman exercised a profound influence on my character and life. While I was a mere boy in my early teens he honored me with his friendship. We often took walks in the country together, and I spent many hours with him at the Parish House, which had just been constructed."

Confirmed at St. Peter's at the age of sixteen, Marshall continued for the rest of his life in the way he had been brought up. Throughout his notable career, Marshall regularly attended church services, and he always tried to build up the churches—both the physical structures and attendance at worship—on the posts to which he was assigned. He ended his days as a faithful communicant of St. James' Episcopal Church in Leesburg, Virginia.

Historians cite the impact of the *Rules of Civility* on George Washington and of Groton headmaster Endicott Peabody on Franklin Roosevelt. With at least as much confidence they should name prayer-book spirituality as a steady influence on George Marshall, not only as a boy but throughout his life. Gradual nurture and slow transformation, rather than an emotional conversion experience, marked his religious journey, guided by the words and actions in the *Book of Common Prayer*.

This text's influence on the language and literature of English-speaking peoples rivaled that of the Authorized Version of the Bible and the works of William Shakespeare. As a boy, Marshall would have been brought up on the 1789 American version of the *Book of Common Prayer*. Its direct descendants were the revisions of 1892 and 1928, in which Marshall would have continued to feel at home. The prayer book would not be rendered into contemporary American English until twenty years after Marshall's death. Its 1662 Church of England form—whose words, also, would have been largely familiar to Marshall—was Edmund Burke's prayer book.

Incorporating large amounts of scripture, prayer-book services were the primary context of Marshall's virtues. This piety oriented his will and shaped his character. A conservative internationalist, Marshall initiated and helped to secure passage of a program for western European recovery that we can at least say was wholly consonant with both his grand strategy as an American statesman and his practice as a faithful churchman.

Former secretary of state Dean Acheson called Marshall the "least militant of soldiers." Indeed, Marshall would have prayed the Collect for Peace, in the Order for Daily Morning Prayer, with complete understanding and in a spirit of heartfelt approbation:

> O God, who art the author of peace and lover of concord, in knowledge of whom standeth our eternal life, whose service is perfect freedom; Defend us thy humble servants in all assaults of our enemies; that we, surely trusting in thy defence, may not fear the power of any adversaries, through the might of Jesus Christ our Lord. Amen.

In his personal history of the Church of England, titled *Our Church*, Roger Scruton analyzes these lines and comments, "The phrase 'whose service is perfect freedom' is a rebuke directed to those who think that freedom and authority are in conflict."

Freedom does not conflict with true authority. In this prayer, Omnipotence and Omniscience ("in knowledge of whom standeth our eternal life") are established as "the author of peace and lover of concord" and hence trustworthy. But even more: God is for us and not against us. We know this truth because in his service lies our perfect freedom. To serve this One liberates our authentic selves. Confidently, therefore, we can ask God to defend us "in all assaults of our enemies," so that, "trusting in thy defence," we may not live in fear.

The prayer books that Burke and Marshall came to know almost by heart included clear statements of human fallenness:

an unpopular theme today, even in churches. The General Confession, which the congregation recited at every service of morning or evening prayer, acknowledged the drag of selfishness on even our best efforts: "We have followed too much the devices and desires of our own hearts." These words reinforced worshipers' sense of humility before God and one another. Burke prized this virtue, affirming its value in the thinking and practice of politicians and statesmen.

The prayer book incorporated another motif besides sinfulness: forgiveness, reconciliation, peace, and, as we have just seen, freedom. This mixture of themes in the *Book of Common Prayer*—sin and grace, tragedy and triumph—amounted to "Christian realism" before the theologian Reinhold Niebuhr made that phrase widely known. Marshall's conservative internationalism incorporated Christian realism.

These themes came together in the regular celebration of the Lord's Supper. Many times Marshall would have participated in the sacrament of Holy Communion. This service had a good bit of humility for believers to take on, especially in the Prayer of Humble Access: "We are not worthy so much as to gather up the crumbs under thy Table." But this same prayer concluded with the petition that we might partake of Christ's body and blood so "that we may evermore dwell in him, and he in us." Dominant was this hopeful theme of incorporation, not only later on, in God's "everlasting kingdom," but also here and now.

Thus this prayer-book rite included a powerful stress on grace as mutual indwelling. After receiving the bread and wine, communicants gave thanks "that we are very members incorporate in the mystical body of thy Son, which is the blessed company of all faithful people." Then they prayed that God would "assist us with thy grace, that we may continue in that holy fellowship, and do all such good works as thou hast prepared for us to walk in; through Jesus Christ our Lord."

Marshall's piety focused first on God as center of value, then on country and family. From George Washington and undoubtedly from other sources and experiences, he learned and took to heart the virtue of duty—answering without wavering when duty called—so that, even when he would have preferred to retire from public life, he still said "yes" to his nation's summons. This sense of responsibility—doing what he knew he ought to do rather than what he would have liked to do—became second nature to him.

This ethical awareness—or, more precisely, this steady purpose—is what Burke, in *Reflections on the Revolution in France*, means by "prejudice," which, he says, "does not leave [a person] hesitating in the moment of decision, sceptical, puzzled, and unresolved." Virtues coalesce to form character so that reliability in moral practice, rather than "a series of disconnected acts," becomes a person's consistent pattern of behavior. In this way, "duty," Burke notes, "becomes a part of [a person's] nature." So it was with General Marshall.

Burke's misgivings about the reigning, liberal understanding of "contract" are well known. Our larger "connexions," to use his word, are decisive. Rather than resembling a contract in civil law, our social relations and obligations ought to be viewed with "reverence" as "a partnership" in knowledge, in art, and "in every virtue." Burke had a profound grasp of social order and of the moral duty that these relations entail: obligation impelled by gratitude.

In his short book *Conservatism: An Invitation to the Great Tradition*, Roger Scruton unfolds the implications of Burke's "defence of the social inheritance." Not contract but trusteeship is what Burke had in mind: "a shared inheritance for the sake of which we learn to circumscribe our demands" and to see our place "as part of a...chain of giving and receiving." Seen from the perspective of trusteeship, "the good things we inherit are not ours to spoil but ours to safeguard." Therefore, Scruton points out, we proceed not by "cost-benefit calculations," as we might if we were deal making prior to a favorable contract, but by "seeing ourselves as inheriting benefits and passing them on." And here is the key point: "Concern for future generations" is an expression of our "gratitude" for what we have received.

Never a regular student of political philosophy, Marshall nonetheless knew in his bones just what Burke had in mind. The American general never forgot what free citizens owe to warriors in a just cause. When in 1953 he accepted the Nobel Peace Prize, he referred to "the cost of war in human lives...constantly spread before me."

Speaking to college students in Frederick, Maryland, in 1951, Marshall urged his listeners to "appreciate" what America means and to "cease to accept as a matter of course your blessings, your rare good fortune." If you do appreciate these gifts, then "you will turn seriously...to the problem of what you personally can do to see that the United States...continues a great democracy and a bulwark of freedom." In these remarks, Marshall identified the single virtue that both inspires an individual's personal contribution and buttresses liberty and constitutional governance because it is the only fitting response to those who secured our freedoms "inch by inch": gratitude.

In a vignette from the Second World War, we can see Marshall's devotion to his family. The human cost of this conflict was brought home to him when he received a radio message on May 30, 1944, from General Mark Clark, commander of the Italian campaign. It informed the Army chief of staff that his stepson, Lieutenant Allen T. Brown, the twenty-seven-year-old son of his wife, Katherine, had been killed in action the previous day near Velletri, south of the Alban Hills, as his tank unit advanced toward Rome. A loving step-father, Marshall was devastated. It was a week before D-Day in France. Following his fact-finding visit to Normandy on the heels of the invasion, Marshall on June 18 visited Allen's grave at the temporary Anzio cemetery, interviewed members of his stepson's crew, flew over the battle terrain in an observation plane, and worked to reconstruct the action surrounding Allen's death at the hands of a German sniper.

In Marshall's life and career, we can easily discern the presence of *pietas*: reverence toward God, country, and kinsmen. And we can detect the elements in his upbringing that shaped *pietas*. His soundly constructed piety ordered his soul, oriented his virtues, and contributed to the common good.

How to Become Virtuous

How can a person become virtuous? By being well informed about what the virtues are, including definitions and examples? By becoming familiar with how good habits work together? By recognizing the natural necessity of the virtues? By analyzing and discussing them in class? By seeing how they apply in different spheres of activity? By going to school on outstanding role models? By being stirred by dramatic representations in fiction and film? By regularly enacting such traits as honesty and generosity, loyalty and courage, temperance and justice? By putting on the hopeful imagination of a friend, teacher, or relative? By attending church regularly? Through prayer and by studying the Bible? By being thankful and loving?

I'd answer: *All that and more.* In the 1662 *Book of Common Prayer*, as well as in all the versions that General Marshall used, the Collect for the Seventeenth Sunday after Trinity reads as follows:

> Lord, we pray thee that thy grace may always prevent and follow us, and make us continually to be given to all good works, through Jesus Christ our Lord. *Amen.*

APPENDIX A

VIRTUES

Theological Virtues

Faith: Belief, trust, and loyalty

Hope: Confident expectation

Love: Deep affection and devotion

Cardinal Virtues

Prudence: Practical wisdom

Justice: Fair play

Courage: Steadfast resolve

Temperance: Self-mastery

Other Virtues

Duty: Obligation

Gratitude: Thankfulness

Honesty: Trustworthiness, truthfulness, straightforwardness

Honor: Ethical responsibility

Humility: Realistic self-awareness, lacking sinful pride

Industry: Hard work

Integrity: Personal wholeness, moral soundness

Loyalty: Fidelity

Magnanimity: Greatness of soul, nobility, not pettiness or meanness

Patience: Attention, endurance, perseverance, relinquishment

Piety: Devotion, dedication, reverence

Stability: Steadiness, composure, abidingness

APPENDIX B

BEACHHEADS

Each institution must take its own approach to teaching the virtues, but all schools that plan to do so would benefit from first establishing a beachhead: a secure starting point for subsequent maneuvers. This beachhead marks the school's commitment to teach the virtues, states its intention to infuse them throughout the school's activities, and identifies which virtues the school deems most important. For example, Saint James School (Maryland) has included the following paragraph in its school handbook:

> Saint James School takes special care to name the traits of moral and spiritual excellence and to infuse these ancient virtues into the full round of student activities. Recognizing that these good habits build lives that are noble and resilient, we teach the virtues not only in chapel but

also through the residential life, athletics, the arts, and the academic curriculum. We stress, in particular, the theological virtues of faith, hope, and love; the cardinal virtues of prudence, justice, courage, and temperance; and such other crucial traits as honesty, kindness, humility, patience, generosity, loyalty, and gratitude.

It is a simple statement, which, like most administrative texts, accomplishes little work on its own. The real effort is, as usual, left to the teachers, coaches, dorm parents, admissions directors, college counselors, and others on the front lines. What should they do?

I am reluctant to say. While strategy points out the goal and the general path, actions in service of strategic goals are most appropriately selected in light of immediate conditions—and therefore should be decided on and implemented by those who are directly familiar with the local terrain, challenges, and capabilities. The Russian and Soviet military strategist Aleksandr Svechin (1878–1938), a victim of the Great Purge, famously observed, "Tactics make the steps from which operational leaps are assembled." In other words, build up operational plans and objectives in relation both to the strategic goal and to tactical opportunities on the ground.

BIBLIOGRAPHY

Acheson, Dean. *Present at the Creation: My Years in the State Department.* New York: Norton, 1969.

Adams, John. *Thoughts on Government, Applicable to the Present State of the American Colonies.* 1776. In *The Political Writings of John Adams: Representative Selections.* Edited by George A. Peek Jr. Indianapolis, IN: Hackett, 2003.

Auchincloss, Louis. *The Rector of Justin.* Boston: Houghton Mifflin, 1964.

Augustine. *Confessions.* Translated by R. S. Pine-Coffin. Harmondsworth, UK: Penguin, 1979.

Backus, Steven. "Freshman Comp Tantrums." *Chronicle of Higher Education*, September 21, 2009.

Berger, Peter. "On the Obsolescence of the Concept of Honor." *European Journal of Sociology* 11 (1970): 339–47.

Bicheno, Hugh. "Washington, Gen. George." In *The Oxford Companion to Military History*. Edited by Richard Holmes. Oxford: Oxford University Press, 2001.

The Book of Common Prayer and Administration of the Sacraments and Other Rites and Ceremonies of the Church. 1789, 1928. New York: Church Pension Fund, 1945.

Booth, T. Michael, and Duncan Spencer. *Paratrooper: The Life of Gen. James M. Gavin*. New York: Simon and Schuster, 1994.

Boswell, James. *The Life of Samuel Johnson*. 1799. Abridged, with an introduction, by Bergen Evans. New York: Modern Library, 1965.

Boyd, Craig A., and Kevin Timpe. *The Virtues: A Very Short Introduction*. Oxford: Oxford University Press, 2021.

Breashears, Caroline. "Education and the English Language." *Law & Liberty* (online), April 10, 2023.

Brookhiser, Richard. *George Washington on Leadership*. New York: Basic, 2008.

Burke, Edmund. "Letter to a Member of the National Assembly." 1791. In *Reflections on the Revolution in France, and Other Writings*. Edited by Jesse Norman. New York: Knopf, 2015.

———. *Reflections on the Revolution in France*. 1790. Edited by Frank M. Turner. New Haven, CT: Yale University Press, 2003.

Burnham, James. *The Managerial Revolution*. Bloomington: Indiana University Press, 1960.

Chernow, Ron. *George Washington: A Life*. New York: Penguin, 2010.

Cicero, Marcus Tullius. *"The Republic" and "The Laws."* Oxford World's Classics. Translated by Niall Rudd. Oxford: Oxford University Press, 1998.

Clark, Kevin, and Ravi Scott Jain. *The Liberal Arts Tradition: A Philosophy of Christian Classical Education*. 3rd ed. Camp Hill, PA: Classical Academic Press, 2021.

Dillon, Brian. "Where You Are Not." *Times Literary Supplement*, no. 5393 (2006): 25.

Dulles, Avery, SJ. "Saving Ecumenism from Itself." *First Things*, no. 178 (2007): 23–27.

Eliot, T. S. *The Idea of a Christian Society*. 1939. In *Christianity and Culture*. New York: Harcourt, 1977.

Ellis, Joseph J. *His Excellency: George Washington*. New York: Vintage, 2004.

———. *The Quartet: Orchestrating the Second American Revolution, 1783–1789*. New York: Knopf, 2015.

Farrer, Austin. *A Celebration of Faith*. London: Hodder and Stoughton, 1972.

———. *Love Almighty and Ills Unlimited: An Essay on Providence and Evil*. London: Collins, 1962.

Fleming, John V. *The Anti-Communist Manifestos: Four Books That Shaped the Cold War.* New York: Norton, 2009.

Foot, Philippa. *Natural Goodness.* Oxford: Clarendon, 2001.

Franklin, Benjamin. "Letter to Messrs. the Abbés Chalut and Arnaud, April 17, 1787." In vol. 10 of *The Works of Benjamin Franklin.* Edited by Jared Sparks. Boston, 1844.

Frohnen, Bruce. *Virtue and the Promise of Conservatism: The Legacy of Burke and Tocqueville.* Lawrence: University Press of Kansas, 1993.

Garfinkle, Adam. "The Erosion of Deep Literacy." *National Affairs*, no. 43 (2020): 192–208.

Garvey, John H. *The Virtues.* Washington, DC: Catholic University of America Press, 2022.

Geach, Peter. *The Virtues.* Cambridge: Cambridge University Press, 1977.

Gini, Al, and Ronald M. Green. *10 Virtues of Outstanding Leaders: Leadership and Character.* Newark, NJ: Wiley, 2013.

Guroian, Vigen. "Seeing Worship as Ethics." In *Incarnate Love: Essays in Orthodox Ethics.* Notre Dame, IN: University of Notre Dame Press, 1989.

The Hanging Tree. Directed by Delmer Daves, Karl Malden, and Vincent Sherman. Warner Bros., 1959. DVD. Burbank, CA: Warner Home Video, 2012.

Harned, David Baily. *Faith and Virtue.* 1973. Eugene, OR: Wipf and Stock, 2020.

———. *Patience: How We Wait Upon the World.* 1997. Rev. ed. Eugene, OR: Wipf and Stock, 2015.

Heckscher, August. *St. Paul's: The Life of a New England School.* New York: Scribner's, 1980.

Hein, David. "Counterpoint to Combat: The Education of Airborne Commander James M. Gavin." *Army* 63, no. 7 (2013): 49–52.

———. "George Washington and the Patience of Power." *Modern Age* 57, no. 4 (2015): 35–43.

———. "The High Church Origins of the American Boarding School." *Journal of Ecclesiastical History* 42 (1991): 577–95.

———. "In War for Peace: General George C. Marshall's Core Convictions and Ethical Leadership." *Touchstone* 26, no. 2 (2013): 41–48.

———. "The Marshall Plan: Conservative Reform as a Weapon of War." *Modern Age* 59, no. 1 (2017): 7–18.

Johnson, Daniel. "The Dereliction of Duty." *New Criterion* 34, no. 5 (2016): 24–29.

Johnson, Dorothy M. *The Hanging Tree.* Lincoln: University of Nebraska Press, 1957.

Johnson, Samuel. *A Dictionary of the English Language.* 2 vols. London, 1755.

Kaczor, Christopher, and Thomas Sherman, SJ. *Thomas Aquinas on the Cardinal Virtues: A Summa of the Summa on Justice, Courage, Temperance, and Practical Wisdom.* Washington, DC: Catholic University of America Press, 2008.

Kierkegaard, Søren. *Purity of Heart Is to Will One Thing.* 1846. Edited and translated by Douglas V. Steere. New York: Harper and Brothers, 1948.

Kirk, Russell. "The Moral Imagination." In *The Essential Russell Kirk: Selected Essays.* Edited by George A. Panichas. Wilmington, DE: ISI Books, 2007.

———. *The Politics of Prudence.* Bryn Mawr, PA: Intercollegiate Studies Institute, 1993.

Knox, James Carter. *Henry Augustus Coit: First Rector of Saint Paul's School, Concord, New Hampshire.* New York: Longmans, Green, 1915.

Koestler, Arthur. *Darkness at Noon.* Trans. Daphne Hardy. New York: Macmillan, 1941.

Lewis, C. S. *The Screwtape Letters.* 1942. New York: Touchstone, 1996.

Lucas, F. L. *Style: The Art of Writing Well.* 1955. Petersfield, UK: Harriman House, 2012.

Lynch, William F., SJ. *Images of Hope.* New York: New American Library, 1965.

MacIntyre, Alasdair. *After Virtue: A Study in Moral Theory.* 3rd ed. Notre Dame, IN: University of Notre Dame Press, 2007.

Marshall, George C. *"The Soldierly Spirit," December 1880–June 1939.* Vol. 1 of *The Papers of George Catlett Marshall.* Edited by Larry I. Bland and Sharon Ritenour Stevens. Baltimore: Johns Hopkins University Press, 1981.

McLachlan, James. *American Boarding Schools: A Historical Study.* New York: Scribner, 1970.

Middlekauff, Robert. *Washington's Revolution: The Making of America's First Leader.* New York: Knopf, 2015.

Milbank, Sebastian. "Deadly Virtues." *First Things,* no. 331 (2023): 12–15.

More, Hannah. *Christian Morals.* 2 vols. London, 1813.

———. *Practical Piety; or, The Influence of the Religion of the Heart on the Conduct of the Life.* 2 vols. London, 1811.

———. *Sacred Dramas: Chiefly Intended for Young Persons.* London, 1782.

———. *Strictures on the Modern System of Female Education.* 2 vols. London, 1799.

———. *Village Politics 1793 with The Shepherd of Salisbury Plain, c. 1820.* Oxford, UK: Woodstock, 1995.

More, Martha. *Mendip Annals; or, A Narrative of the Charitable Labours of Hannah More and Martha More in Their Neighbourhood.* Edited by Arthur Roberts. London, 1859.

Morrow, Lance. "The Danger of Debating Reparations." *Wall Street Journal,* May 3, 2019.

Niebuhr, H. Richard. *Radical Monotheism and Western Culture, with Supplementary Essays*. 1960. Louisville, KY: Westminster/John Knox Press, 1993.

Niebuhr, Reinhold. *The Children of Light and the Children of Darkness: A Vindication of Democracy and a Critique of Its Traditional Defense*. New York: Scribner, 1960.

Nisbet, Robert. *The Quest for Community: A Study in the Ethics of Order and Freedom*. 1953. Rev. ed. Wilmington, DE: ISI Books, 2010.

Norrell, Robert J. *Up from History: The Life of Booker T. Washington*. Cambridge, MA: Harvard University Press, 2009.

Oakeshott, Michael. *The Voice of Liberal Learning*. 1989. Indianapolis, IN: Liberty Fund, 2001.

———. "The Voice of Poetry in the Conversation of Mankind." In *Rationalism in Politics, and Other Essays*. Carmel, IN: Liberty Fund, 1991.

O'Keefe, Mark, OSB. *Virtues Abounding: St. Thomas Aquinas on the Cardinal and Related Virtues for Today*. Eugene, OR: Cascade, 2019.

Orwell, George. "Why I Write." 1946. In *Why I Write*. New York: Penguin, 2005.

Peltz, Lucy. "'A Revolution in Female Manners': Women, Politics, and Reputation in the Late Eighteenth Century." In *Brilliant Women: Eighteenth-Century Bluestockings*. Edited by Elizabeth Eger and Lucy Peltz. New Haven, CT: Yale University Press, 2008.

Pieper, Josef. *The Four Cardinal Virtues*. Notre Dame, IN: University of Notre Dame Press, 1966.

Pinker, Steven. *The Sense of Style: The Thinking Person's Guide to Writing in the Twenty-First Century*. New York: Viking, 2014.

Plato. *Protagoras and Meno*. Translated by Adam Beresford. London: Penguin, 2005.

———. *The Republic*. Translated by Francis Macdonald Cornford. New York: Oxford University Press, 1972.

Pogue, Forrest C. *George C. Marshall: Organizer of Victory, 1943–1945*. New York: Viking, 1973.

Prior, Karen Swallow. *Fierce Convictions: The Extraordinary Life of Hannah More; Poet, Reformer, Abolitionist*. Nashville, TN: Nelson Books, 2014.

Ride the High Country. Directed by Sam Peckinpah. Metro-Goldwyn-Mayer, 1962. DVD. Burbank, CA: Turner Entertainment Corp. and Warner Bros. Entertainment, Inc., 2006.

Robertson, Frederick W. *Sermons on Religion and Life*. New York: E. P. Dutton, 1906.

Rose, Phyllis. *The Shelf: From LEQ to LES; Adventures in Extreme Reading*. New York: Farrar, Straus and Giroux, 2014.

Rousseau, Jean-Jacques. *The First and Second Discourses*. Edited by Roger D. Masters. Translated by Roger D. Masters and Judith R. Masters. Boston: St. Martin's Press, 1964.

Saint Augustine's Prayer Book. 1947. Rev. ed. Edited by David Cobb. Cincinnati, OH: Forward Movement for the Order of the Holy Cross, 2014.

Scammell, Michael. Introduction to *Darkness at Noon*, by Arthur Koestler. Translated by Philip Boehm. London: Vintage, 2019.

Scruton, Roger. *Against the Tide: The Best of Roger Scruton's Columns, Commentaries, and Criticism*. Edited by Mark Dooley. London: Bloomsbury, 2022.

———. *Conservatism: An Invitation to the Great Tradition*. New York: All Points, 2018.

———. *Our Church: A Personal History of the Church of England*. London: Atlantic, 2012.

Scruton, Roger, and Mark Dooley. *Conversations with Roger Scruton*. London: Bloomsbury Continuum, 2016.

Sheen, Fulton J. "The Fifth Word and the Virtue of Temperance." In *The Seven Last Words*. Garden City, NY: Garden City Books, 1952.

Skinner, David. "Craft Warning." *Washington Examiner*, October 23, 2014.

Smith, James K. A. *Desiring the Kingdom: Worship, Worldview, and Cultural Formation*. Vol. 1 of *Cultural Liturgies*. Grand Rapids, MI: Baker Academic, 2009.

Sokolowski, Robert. *The God of Faith and Reason: Foundations of Christian Theology*. 1982. Washington, DC: Catholic University of America Press, 1995.

Sommers, Christina Hoff. "Teaching the Virtues." *Imprimis* (Hillsdale College) 20, no. 11 (1991): 1–5.

Sowell, Thomas. *Black Rednecks and White Liberals.* New York: Encounter, 2005.

Stott, Anne. *Hannah More: The First Victorian.* New York: Oxford University Press, 2003.

Swaim, Barton. *The Speechwriter: A Brief Education in Politics.* New York: Simon and Schuster, 2015.

Tocqueville, Alexis de. *Democracy in America.* 2 vols. 1835, 1840. Edited by Eduardo Nolla. Translated by James T. Schleifer. Carmel, IN: Liberty Fund, 2010.

Underhill, Evelyn. *Ruysbroeck.* London: G. Bell, 1915.

Vanstone, W. H. *The Stature of Waiting.* London: Darton, Longman and Todd, 1982.

Voegelin, Eric. *The New Science of Politics: An Introduction.* 1952. Chicago: University of Chicago Press, 1987.

Warren, Robert Penn. *All the King's Men.* 1946. New York: Houghton Mifflin Harcourt, 1996.

Washington, Booker T. "The Negro and the Labor Unions." *Atlantic Monthly* 111 (1913): 756–67.

———. "Speech for the Cotton States and International Exposition in Atlanta, Georgia, September 18, 1895." In vol. 3 of *The Booker T. Washington Papers.* Edited by Louis R. Harlan. Urbana: University of Illinois Press, 1974.

———. *Up from Slavery.* 1901. Mineola, NY: Dover, 1995.

———. *Working with the Hands.* New York: Doubleday, 1904.

Washington, George. *Writings.* Edited by John Rhodehamel. New York: Library of America, 1997.

Weaver, Richard M. *The Ethics of Rhetoric.* Brattleboro, VT: Echo Point, 1953.

Weil, Simone. "Attention and Will." In *Gravity and Grace.* 1947. London: Routledge, 2002.

Whittaker, John H. *Matters of Faith and Matters of Principle: Religious Truth Claims and Their Logic.* San Antonio, TX: Trinity University Press, 1981.

Wister, Owen. "Dr. Coit of St. Paul's." *Atlantic Monthly* 142 (1928): 756–68.

Wolf, Maryanne. *Reader, Come Home: The Reading Brain in a Digital World.* New York: Harper, 2018.

Wood, Gordon S. *Revolutionary Characters: What Made the Founders Different.* New York: Penguin, 2006.

Zinsser, William. *On Writing Well: The Classic Guide to Writing Nonfiction.* 7th ed. New York: Harper, 2016.

ACKNOWLEDGMENTS

Perhaps you won't mind if a seasoned professor does some reminiscing. The direct antecedents of this little book are a couple of pieces having to do with writing. For both my undergraduate and my postgraduate students, I used to hand out and discuss a five-page photocopied item that I unimaginatively titled "Advice to Paper Writers." This document consisted of excellent quotations from all sorts of writers, teachers, and editors. You will have come across a number of these selections in this book's Chapter 3. I believe that the subtext of my handout was that the course instructor's approach to assessing prose style and content was not completely idiosyncratic: all good readers are remarkably alike in the qualities they expect to see in nonfiction writing and in the flaws they hope to avoid.

One day, after rereading the quotations in my handout more carefully, I realized two facts: One was that implicit in most of these remarks were virtues pertaining to good writing. The other was that the phrase *ethics and writing* calls to mind or summons from the internet a limited range of material: mainly, advice on avoiding plagiarism and employing inclusive language.

Consequently, I took the good counsel and often witty, incisive sentences from "Advice to Paper Writers" and made an article out of them: "Writing as a Moral Act," first published in the *Imaginative Conservative* on August 30, 2021. From time to time, this piece reappears on the *Imaginative Conservative* website as a Timeless Essay. One of the appealing features of the internet is that it often allows readers to comment immediately on an author's work. Readers of this article appeared to find some value in it.

One of the readers who appreciated this essay was Dr. Jeffrey O. Nelson, cofounder and executive director of the Russell Kirk Center for Cultural Renewal, in Mecosta, Michigan. He invited me to Piety Hill, the amazing home of the late Russell Kirk, the author of *The Conservative Mind* and *The Roots of American Order*, to teach a short seminar and workshop called "Writing and the Moral Imagination" in the summer of 2023. Delightful, talented students turned up from all over the United States. Hosted by Annette Y. Kirk, who embodies the Christian virtue of hospitality, we had a wonderful time. What these smart, thoroughly engaging and engaged young people revealed was a strong interest in both writing and the virtues.

Then, in the fall and spring terms of 2023–24, I led professional-development sessions at Saint James School, near Hagerstown, Maryland, on infusing the virtues into the curriculum of a traditional church school. These experiences gave both my thinking and my enthusiasm a big boost, and

I am grateful to the headmaster, the Reverend Dr. D. Stuart Dunnan; to the associate head and academic dean, Mrs. Kimberly Kingry; and to the outstanding Saint James faculty for their welcome and support. Meanwhile, I continued to try out my ideas in short essays in such periodicals as the *Living Church*, the *Salisbury Review*, and *VoegelinView*.

A friend of nearly a half century, Professor Vigen Guroian, Permanent Senior Fellow at the Russell Kirk Center, urged me to do a book on these themes. He assured me that a primer on teaching and the virtues did not yet exist and was sorely needed. I warmly appreciate Vigen's encouragement and steadfast support.

Eventually, these pieces on teaching and curriculum started to flow together in my mind with work I had pursued for more than forty years on the virtues of great leaders. In 1982 my dissertation on Abraham Lincoln's faith and political ethics was completed at the University of Virginia under the supervision of Professor Kenneth W. Thompson. More recently, I spent six years as a senior fellow at the George C. Marshall Foundation, in Lexington, Virginia, helping to relaunch the foundation's highly regarded undergraduate scholars program. This association stimulated my research and reflections on General Marshall, a premier strategist and diplomat, who had first been introduced to me—with enthusiasm—by Professor Thompson, an expert in ethics and foreign policy.

And yet the actual roots of this book lie much deeper, and I shall not be able to unearth all of them. As I write about in Chapter 2, my first lesson in applied ethics was given to me by my fourth-grade football coach. And, truth be told, if we are the children of loving mothers and fathers, then our training in the virtues begins in the first hours after we are born.

My undergraduate adviser, David Baily Harned, makes precisely this point in his book *Faith and Virtue*, in a chapter in which he challenges—calling it a "misconstruction"—the customary distinction between "theological" and "natural" virtues. Although I believe there is more to be said in favor of the traditional understanding of the theological virtues than Harned does (see, for example, Robert Sokolowski, *The God of Faith and Reason*), I like what he says about the origins of these habits.

As I discuss in Chapter 6, it's the so-called natural virtues like patience and duty that strike most of us as unnatural. Harned believes that the theological virtues, on the other hand, "are the commonest of all human phenomena, familiar as laughter or hunger or sleep, and they inform every significant relationship…with other selves, communities, institutions, and with the earth itself." From his or her first moments, the child of devoted parents begins to learn the habit of basic trust. "Family and friends," Harned observes, "elicit the trust and loyalty that are the primary ingredients of faith, their presence establishing a realm of basic trust within which the child is free to test his powers, dare to dream, risk a fall." My own mother and father deserve more thanks than I can give them, but at least they receive a brief, heartfelt mention in Chapter 6.

My scholarly interest in schools began in 1983, at the end of my first—and only—year teaching English and coaching three sports at a boys' boarding school in the mountains of Virginia. This experience made me curious about the beginnings of my own school, which led to an article in the *Maryland Historical Magazine* called "The Founding of the Boys' School of St. Paul's Parish, Baltimore."

Although I loved my old school and kept in touch with my former teachers, I concluded that there was nothing terribly historic about the place. But the College of St. James (now Saint James School), mentioned in Chapter 2, was different; it played a pivotal role in the rise of the church boarding school. At the Maryland Historical Society, in Baltimore, I uncovered some letters by a student who had been at this school during a fraught period. This edited collection was published as *Religion and Politics in Maryland on the Eve of the Civil War: The Letters of W. Wilkins Davis.*

My inquiry then broadened to include all the prototypical American church boarding schools, such as St. Paul's School in Concord, New Hampshire. My thesis was that previous accounts of their formative periods were incomplete. I found considerable evidence to support the claim that theological ideas—overlooked by historians of education—played a crucial role in their development. This research culminated in "The High Church Origins of the American Boarding School," which appeared in the *Journal of Ecclesiastical History* in 1991.

Over the decades, too, I have been involved with church-related secondary schools as a friend, trustee, occasional speaker, and presenter at the odd conference. I am convinced that these institutions have an indispensable role to play in the formation of the minds and hearts of young people. Hence my ongoing interest in and commitment to their endeavors.

At the Russell Kirk Center, I should like to thank the following three remarkable individuals, each an embodiment of what humane conservatism really means: Emily Corwin, the events coordinator who graciously and capably makes conferences run so well—and yet not "like clockwork" at all, but instead smoothly, warmly, humanly. Annette Kirk: charming and smart, grounded and engaging; it is an honor to know and a pleasure to spend time with her. Jeff Nelson: knowledgeable and imaginative, deeply moral and thoroughly personable, a most enjoyable and trustworthy companion on this journey.

A word of appreciation, as well, to Dr. Roberta L. Bayer, a professor of political philosophy at Patrick Henry College, in Purcellville, Virginia, and former editor of the *Anglican Way*. I am grateful to this esteemed teacher and scholar for contributing the foreword to this volume. Thanks, also, to her and to her husband, Tom, for welcoming me to their home in Paeonian Springs, Virginia, where I have enjoyed relaxed suppers and good company in beautiful, historic surroundings.

Special thanks to Professor Mark Sandona for preparing the bibliography, for reading and commenting on the manuscript, and for excellent conversations on vice and virtue and on much in between.

Thanks, also, to my friend and adviser John Reim, who offered timely wisdom on the virtue of piety, particularly in relation to formal prayer.

Grateful acknowledgment is made to the following outlets, in which portions of my work appeared before being mined for the present effort: *American National Biography*, *Army* magazine, the *Christian Century*, the *Imaginative Conservative*, the *Intercollegiate Review*, the *Journal of Ecclesiastical History*, the *Living Church*, *Marshall* magazine (George C. Marshall Foundation), *Modern Age*, *Providence: A Journal of Christianity and American Foreign Policy*, *Religion & Liberty Online*, the *Salisbury Review*, *The Statesman* (John Jay Institute), *Touchstone*, and *VoegelinView*.

INDEX

Note: Illustrations are indicated by page numbers in *italics*.

ABOUT THE AUTHOR

David Hein is Distinguished Teaching Fellow at the Russell Kirk Center for Cultural Renewal. He earned his PhD from the University of Virginia and has extensive teaching experience at the high school and college levels. Hein serves as a trustee of Saint James School (Maryland) and of the George C. Marshall Foundation. He is the author or coauthor of five other books, and he writes frequently for the *New Criterion*, *Modern Age*, *Touchstone*, the *Journal of Military History*, *Army*, the *Journal of Ecclesiastical History*, and other publications.

ABOUT THE TYPE

This book is set in Adobe Caslon, a digital typeface that Carol Twombly designed in 1990. Twombly created this type after studying pages that William Caslon printed in England between 1734 and 1770. Caslon's types, based on seventeenth-century Dutch old-style designs, became popular throughout Europe and in America. In fact, the first printings of the American Declaration of Independence and the Constitution were set in Caslon.

ABOUT THE PUBLISHER

Mecosta House publishes beautiful and accessible books that conserve timeless wisdom pertinent to every age. It is the imprint of the Russell Kirk Center for Cultural Renewal.

The Russell Kirk Center aims to recover, conserve, and enliven those enduring norms and principles that Russell Kirk (1918–1994) called the Permanent Things.

MECOSTA
— H O U S E —   1

www.ingramcontent.com/pod-product-compliance
Lightning Source LLC
Chambersburg PA
CBHW030825090426
42737CB00009B/877